I BELIEVE THIS

Some of John Marsden's titles

The Boy You Brought Home
Secret Men's Business
Everything I Know About Writing
Tomorrow, When the War Began
This I Believe (ed.)
For Weddings and a Funeral (ed.)
Prayer for the 21st Century
The Rabbits
So Much To Tell You
Letters From the Inside
Winter
Checkers
The Journey
Marsden on Marsden
A Roomful of Magic

I BELIEVE THIS

100 EMINENT AUSTRALIANS FACE LIFE'S BIGGEST QUESTION

EDITED BY

JOHN MARSDEN

RANDOM HOUSE AUSTRALIA

Random House Australia Pty Ltd
20 Alfred Street, Milsons Point, NSW 2061
http://www.randomhouse.com.au

Sydney   New York   Toronto
London   Auckland   Johannesburg

First published by Random House Australia 2004

National Library of Australia
Cataloguing-in-Publication Entry

Marsden, John, 1950–.
I believe this.

ISBN 1 74051 254 5.

1. Australians – Attitudes. 2. Spiritual life. I. Title.

303.38

Cover photograph © Sonya Pletes
Cover design by Michelle Macintosh
Typeset in Arial and Bembo by Midland Typesetters, Maryborough, Victoria
Printed and bound by Griffin Press, Netley, South Australia

10 9 8 7 6 5 4 3 2 1

Royalties from the sale of this book are being donated to Save the Children Fund
Australia. Save the Children Fund is an international aid, development and advocacy
agency, working for a better world with children. Save the Children Fund aims to
ensure that all children, regardless of gender, race, country of origin or religious
belief have the means for survival, receive protection, and have access to nutrition,
primary health care and basic education.

For Harriet Alexander
(this too can be an island)

ACKNOWLEDGEMENTS

Thanks to Jane Palfreyman, Roberta Ivers, Katie Stackhouse, Michelle Mitchell, Anyez Lindop, and Jane Novak.

CONTENTS

Introduction   xi

Contents

INTRODUCTION

It's not so difficult to work out what we don't believe in. Everything from a political party to a particular religion, to the man in the moon. Our daily conversation often includes big slabs of 'what we don't believe in'.

And some people are very clear on what they do believe in. Adherents to religions or political parties or other groups that include belief among their tenets often take on the full kit and caboodle. If certain aspects make them a little uncomfortable they either rationalise them away or make the compromise and accept them.

In a national crisis many people write to newspapers and ring talkback radio to say, in effect, 'the government knows what they are doing . . . they have information that we don't . . . we have to leave them to it, and trust them to make the best decision'.

An unquestioning belief in authority means that they do not need to bring their own thinking and experience and knowledge to a situation but instead can assign the responsibility to others.

Equally, a belief held 'under orders' is not much of a belief.

I suspect that if we probed deep into the origins of all laws we would find a contempt for human beings: a suspicion that we are not capable of living moral and generous lives if left to ourselves. I think this contempt is at the heart of governments, political parties and organised religions.

To consider and articulate one's own beliefs, rather than lazily talk about what we don't believe in, is unusual in our society. In 1949 one hundred eminent citizens of the UK did it for a book called *This I Believe*. As a teenager I found this book intensely interesting and in 1996 I asked one hundred eminent Australians to write about their beliefs for a book with the same title: *This I Believe*.

Now, with a significant darkening of the world in the last few years it seemed like a good idea to do it again.

I invited Australians from all states, of all ages, of both genders, with skills ranging from choreography to surviving on the streets, from surgery to playwriting, and achievements ranging from 'Australian of the Year' to a Tony, a Mo, an AWGIE, an Emmy and the Women's Electoral Lobby Edna Ryan Award for Humour to take on this onerous task. And I included half a dozen young people who were not yet 'eminent' in the generally accepted meaning of the word.

The response was generous and positive. The essays started to arrive. For me, some were inspiring, some compelling, some annoying, some moving.

As with the first book though, business leaders, and politicians, with a few shining exceptions, were disgracefully absent. Their excuse was always the same: 'I'm too busy'.

All of the people I invited to contribute to this book were busy. I think there has to be some other reason for the absence of business leaders and politicians.

But one hundred people took the trouble to sit down and think through what they believe in and why they believe it.

On your behalf, my behalf, and on behalf of the Save the Children Fund, I thank them.

John Marsden
Melbourne, June 2004

Debra Adelaide

Debra Adelaide is the author of two novels, *The Hotel Albatross* and *Serpent Dust*, and has edited several collections of fiction and non-fiction, the latest of which is *Acts of Dog*, published by Random House in November 2003. She spent four years as the *Sydney Morning Herald*'s weekly 'In Short' book reviewer, and now works full-time as a lecturer in writing at the University of Technology, Sydney. She is also writing another novel.

Kink-free hoses

Is it alarming or salutary to discover that as age advances, the preoccupation with moral and ethical certainties recedes?

Sometimes it seems I am no longer capable of holding firm beliefs about anything but the practical and the palpable. Sometimes it seems my greatest passions are aroused when I am doing something quite prosaic. Like watering the garden (oh yes, I believe in water restrictions too, and I do water responsibly). But I fervently believe that a civilisation capable of putting a man on the moon should also be able to invent a kink-free hose. The overwhelming force of this belief strikes me every time I'm doing the gardening. Almost knocked sideways, usually in the direction of the compost, by the force of my anger every time I grapple to unkink a hose that clearly in another life was a corkscrew, I wonder yet again about the ineffectual nature of my complaints upon Them.

The Others. Them. They. As in, They ought to invent a/ improve the/ revise the/ rescind the/ move the/ change the/ restore the [insert here the product or service of your choice]. In my opinion They only need to invent and possibly improve, and life would be vastly depressurised/simplified/pacified. At least, I believe this would be the case. Since belief is frequently a leap of faith into the unknown, so far the inventions or improvements I fantasise about constitute the completely unknown.

Call me unimaginative, but I do believe that a hose that never again kinks to stop the flow of water just at a crucial moment in the watering would be more useful than a moon landing. Thus I may be a ploddingly dull sort of person, but I also believe that the following could only make life smoother:

Mould-free strollers (currently they seem to have spores inbuilt at the factory); self-cleaning refrigerators (they already have ovens that purport to do this, not that I've ever encountered one), and possibly also car interiors; snail- and slug-proof letterboxes (or at least gastropods genetically modified to prefer Big W catalogues over pay cheques); at least *one* fat-free product (there are 374 in my supermarket) that tastes like the promised real thing (and yes, I can believe it's not butter, in fact I believe it's recycled suntan oil); TVs that are sold already programmed, requiring neither children nor degrees in electronics to operate; kitchen scissors that never disappear; and a washing machine whose cycle includes the return of the other sock.

Humble, domestic desires, all these. Not impossible things like dent-proof cars, cures for cancer, or computers that do not become obsolete within a month. But I could if pressed speculate about these too. Pain-free dental treatment. The alignment of train timetables with train movements. Self-completing tax returns, not to mention refunds of more than three figures . . . I believe a culture clever enough to invent the Internet, imaginative enough to operate toy trucks on Mars, and creative enough to reattach severed penises and graft ears onto the backs of mice could do this.

What else do I believe? All government ministers should work one day a week in a supermarket checkout or at a call centre; they should also all have to read one book a week. Artists and writers should receive a basic living wage. Working mothers should have free home help. That quaint service once known as public funded education should be restored to us. The baker should deliver bread once more. Likewise the milkman. The Higher School Certificate should be exterminated at once. Children should be in bed by eight. And I deserve a vodka and lime every evening at six.

DON AITKIN

Don Aitkin, AO, is a retired Vice-Chancellor (University of Canberra, 1991–2002) who finds himself just as busy in 'retirement', where he spent six months of that long-awaited release serving as the CEO of a R&D company. He is the Chairman of the Boards of the Cultural Facilities Corporation, the Australian Mathematics Trust, the NRMA/ACT Road Safety Trust, and Pro Musica Inc. He has a continuing role with the Canada Foundation for Innovation as well as a number of Australian organisations interested in education, research, urban development, and governance, matters about which he has strong views, and on the whole unorthodox ones. He is a Fellow of the Academy of the Social Sciences in Australia, the Australian College of Education and the Australian Planning Institute. He was the first Chairman of the Australian Research Council (1988–1990), where he trebled the budget and established the ARC as an organisation of world class; he served for six years as a member of the Australian Science and Technology Council (1996–2002).

A historian and political scientist, he was a professor at Macquarie University (1971–1979) and the ANU (1980–1988), and the author of a number of books on Australian politics as well as a novel. He was also a widely read newspaper columnist in the *National Times* and the *Canberra Times*, a contributing editor of *Newsweek*, and a television and radio

commentator. In what passes for his spare time he writes
books and plays the piano.

I tried a few times, but I really didn't ever leave the
education system. I started in it in 1942, at kindergarten in Newcastle, and retired from it in 2002 as
the Vice-Chancellor of the University of Canberra.
Along the way I experienced a primary school, two
high schools, four universities in Australia and three
overseas. I chaired an enquiry into the legislation
governing school education, and at other times I
chaired a number of bodies whose purpose was to
distribute large amounts of money for research. It has
been a rich, enjoyable and always interesting life.

And out of it I learned one enormously important truth, which shapes the way I think about the
world. It is this: *Everyone is born intelligent.* Or put
it another way: *Just about anyone can become anything
they want to be, if they are properly encouraged, motivated
and prepared.* It is not the want of intelligence that
prevents people succeeding, but the lack of those
other attributes of life.

How do I know this? Well, when I started at
university only 2 per cent of my age group went
there, and we were thought to be the 'bright' kids.
Today, about 50 per cent of the same age group go to
university, though more would like to, and some will
go later. Over fifty years I have watched the propor-
tion of students entering university increase, and I've
taught some of them. In my judgment, the students
of today are better than we were. They are about

a year older, their knowledge is broader and their self-confidence is higher.

But they're not 'brighter', only better motivated, better prepared and more generally encouraged (by parents, school and society) to keep learning and aspire to go to university. Incidentally, exit examinations (the Higher School Certificate or its equivalents) and university are both tougher and more searching than they were in my day, too.

There's no good reason why everyone shouldn't aspire to a university education. But you need to be motivated, encouraged and prepared. The same is true about playing tennis, or singing, or skiing. These are all learned skills. Yes, some people have no trouble in hitting the ball effectively, just as some find singing easy and others don't instantly fall over when they put on skis for the first time. But the truth is that if you want to be a good tennis player, and you find a good teacher, and you practise and practise, you will be an excellent tennis player. It isn't true that some people lack hand–eye coordination, or balance, or an 'ear'. We all do, but it's quite easy for us to play down our skills and capacities if they are not well developed. No one wants to appear a dummy when others are plainly proficient. And we only have one life: to be very good at anything requires large amounts of time, energy and sacrifice.

All this means that I try not to categorise people as 'bright' or 'dim'. No one is good at everything – no one has time to be. It also means that I am one of those who tries to help the late developers, partly because we all are late developers in one or more aspects of our lives! It means that I am an egalitarian not an elitist, since I recognise that while people may be wonderfully developed in one activity they will be, necessarily, undeveloped in others. Finally, it means that my urge is always to equalise life chances: we all deserve the opportunity to develop at least some of our capacities.

Need more persuading? Read Howard Gardner's *Frames of Mind*. It's a great book.

HARRIET ALEXANDER

Harriet Alexander wrote this essay in 2003 when she was fourteen and spending a residential school term at King Island, a remote island off the coast of Tasmania. Her school, Ballarat and Clarendon College, runs the King Island campus as part of their Year 9 program for all students.

Harriet's experiences on King Island had a profound effect on her. She sailed, hiked (including a nine-day hike around the entire island), participated in a scientific penguin study, shopped and cooked with her six house-mates within a set budget, created a mosaic, scuba-dived and even learned to knit.

The emphasis on personal growth combined with cooperating in a group to accomplish daily tasks gave Harriet an opportunity that she found both fulfilling and confronting.

Her beliefs continue to alter and adjust as she moves through her teenage years.

I believe that life can be changed in a single moment. That realisation of yourself is a beautiful and terrifying thing. I believe that it is human nature to never be completely satisfied with who you are. Life often seems to be full of need and desire. I desire happiness. I want to be everything that I'm not. I want to achieve, because everyone expects me to. I hate that people see me the way I wish I could.

I'm tired of wishing there was more, of worrying about life and its possibilities. I'm tired of beating myself up and hurting myself. I'm tired of being indecisive. I've had enough.

What do I believe?

I believe sometimes you need time to think about what you have. Someone once asked me what made me happy. I found myself taking a long time to answer.

I believe that people can get too bogged down in themselves and it can be so hard and desperately lonely to surface. The world seems too busy for just one person sometimes. There is so much pain. There is war and famine and hatred. I read last year about people in India called the Untouchables. These people are treated like vermin. One story really struck me. There were two men who tried to make a statement about their rights and went fishing in a pond used by upper caste villagers in Uttar Pradesh. A mob doused the two untouchables with acid. They are disfigured, one half of the older man's face melted into his chin. When I hear these things, that is when I feel most lost. Like there is no hope for humanity. People are cruel.

And then I lose sight. I start to hate humanity, yet accept that I am, after all, a part of it. So I feel guilty. I feel like it's all my fault. All my fault.

So I spend my life apologising. And every time I do, I feel that I'm apologising for existing. But there is always one person I always forget to apologise to. Me. Sometimes I have such a sickening feeling of self loathing I can't breathe. I believe that's unhealthy and needs changing.

I believe you need to trust. I believe somehow, magically, there are these amazing people that pass through your life and make if beautiful. I believe you need people. I believe that the media is so busy spurting out news of all the crap and hardship that goes on, it forgets to mention the good things. Simple things. Rain hammering on a tin roof. A friend that touches you so deeply it is almost terri-fying. There have been three people in my life who have truly inspired me. They've made me want to be alive.

I think sometimes society makes life seem so very lonely and miserable. There is so much pressure and so many lies. I don't want to be alone.

I believe words are the most powerful gift on earth. And I think we should not be afraid to use them. I believe it is a special thing to have someone who will share their theories on life with you, no matter how much they scare you in their truth and sincerity. A person who will make you think and feel worthwhile. A person who is honest.

I believe that I need to smile more. To just smile and laugh. Because it is a good feeling and some-times it's almost as if I am afraid of doing it. Like I'm forcing myself to be miserable. Thriving on self-pity and sadness because it's all I think I have left. I think sometimes you can go numb to all other emotions. Hide yourself away from them because you are afraid. You are afraid to embark on the search for happiness, because maybe you are searching for something that is not there.

Yet I believe that there are things that are worth something in my life. People. I believe in things I have learned, been told and experienced. I've experienced good and bad; life seems to be made up of simply good and bad. And often, a hell of a lot of fear. What I believe and what I do seem different at times. I know what I need to do and I'm going to try and do it. I have to. Because everyone needs to believe. If there is nothing to believe in then life is just an empty period of time. It has to be lived, not endured. And I have learned to make myself believe something I have struggled with every day.

I believe it's not my fault.

I believe you can't live life feeling guilty. Life is full of need and desire. I believe, to be happy, you have to work out what the right thing to need is. The healthy desire. And I believe humans have to believe in themselves. Outside factors are irrelevant. It's a journey of solitude, but one you cannot make alone. It is confusion and clarity. It is need and content-ment. I know what I need. I need to believe in myself.

Taj Aldin Alhilali

Imam Taj Aldin Alhilali is the spiritual leader of Australia's Muslim community, holding the position of Mufty of Australia for the past fifteen years. He is sixty-three years of age and married with four children. An Imam of forty years, he has worked at different mosques in Egypt, Libya, Lebanon and Australia and taught Islamic Studies at University level. He is an appointed member of the nine-member International Council for Islamic Call, and the Ecumenical Council for Sectarian Reconciliation, Iran. He has championed women's rights throughout his life and has established the Muslim Women's Association. His Eminence is a keen sportsman who enjoys athletics, soccer and volleyball. He has also written a number of Islam related books and articles.

I believe that there is one God, the Creator of everyone and everything. God has all the beautiful names and sublime attributes.

I believe that personal freedom stops where the rights of others begin. Therefore, in the interest of social harmony, we must all check our own actions and behaviours so as not to infringe on the freedoms of others. I believe in the Divine teachings that God sent through His messengers and believe that these teachings were sent as an act of Grace to help people better organise their lives. I believe that these instructions and Divine laws are in the best interest of society and that when God told us not to kill, God in fact gave us life; when God told us not to steal, God gave us security. This makes religious teachings like the brakes on a vehicle; without them, one keeps crashing and hurting others.

I believe that the purpose of my life is to arrive to God the Creator with faith and a good record. To do so, I must believe in the teachings of the final book that God sent to us through His final messenger Muhammad, peace and blessings upon him. I believe this book includes comprehensive guidance from God and maintains the ethical teachings of the great men of God such as Noah, Abraham, Moses and Christ. I believe that the Qur'an is the final message from Heaven, a message of love, respect, peace and societal harmony. I believe that traversing through life in accordance with the teachings of this message will help me achieve my goal and win the pleasure of my Creator.

As my Creator is wiser and better informed than I am, I believe that my Creator is the best One to instruct me how to live my life. I believe that the message of the Creator is the best charter for people to live by.

I believe that religion gives us a second safety check to gauge our own actions, so that we adhere to the ethical standards that please God because we believe that God is constantly aware and always sees all that we do.

I believe that we, as human beings, with our

different colours, diverse cultures and languages all come from the same father and mother, Adam and Eve, and that our Creator is One. I believe that the teachings of the Qur'an aim to nurture and protect a person's faith, soul, mind, honour, safety and property. I believe that every person has the right to choose his own religion and that there cannot be any compulsion in religion. I believe that human life is sacred and that anyone who takes life unjustly is offending God. I believe that it is wrong to obscure the human mind with alcohol or drugs. I also believe that theft and deception are wrong.

I believe that Islam is not a religion that was created by Muhammad, peace and blessings upon him, but rather, the way of Islam is the way of all the prophets and messengers of God and that Muhammad came to complement the earlier messages and continue the mission of his predecessors in guiding people towards God.

I believe that the meaning of Islam is to surrender to God and to embrace and promote every aspect of peace in its general comprehensive meaning, peace with God, peace with oneself, peace with our fellow human beings, peace with every other living thing and finally, peace with the environment.

I believe that God created many forms of intelligent life, some with free will, like humans and Jinn, and some without free will, like angels.

I believe in all the prophets and messengers of God and that they were all sent for one purpose, to guide people towards their Creator and to show people the path to goodness, cooperation and the promotion of love and friendship.

I believe that people who believe in religion must work towards better mutual understanding and respect and that any conflict amongst them is a result of a misunderstanding of the purpose and meaning of religion.

I believe in the day of judgement, where God will be the Only Judge and will honour the faithful and punish those who committed evil and transgressions in this world.

I believe that all people are siblings in their humanity and that no race is better than another, that the degree of goodness of a person is based on this person's faith and service to humanity.

I believe that having different religious beliefs is natural and is a catalyst for dialogue and discovery.

I believe that the greatest Jihad is to speak the truth in the face of adversity and to struggle against lust, greed and envy.

DENNIS ALTMAN

Dennis Altman is Professor of Politics at Latrobe University and author of ten books, most recently *Global Sex*. He is currently writing a book called *Gore Vidal's America*. Altman is also President of the AIDS Society of Asia and the Pacific. In 2005 he will take up the position of Visiting Professor of Australian Studies at Harvard University.

Those of us who live in Australia are remarkably lucky. With some exceptions, we take for granted a level of affluence and freedom that is only a mirage for the great majority of people in the world. Nothing underlines this more sharply than the deplorable way in which we currently treat desperate people who seek refuge on our shores (the definition of which itself changes as the government seeks to excise land, and with it the people who land there).

I believe that our luck is both a challenge and an obligation. Increasingly we are adopting views of the world that define us as basically selfish, concerned only with ourselves or at best our immediate family. I believe that we have a responsibility to think more broadly, if only because our own welfare, whether as individuals, as families, or as a country, is bound up with larger concerns.

More specifically I believe:

That humans are capable of both cruelty and generosity, and we must always aim for the best. There are countless examples of human brutality, ranging from genocide in Germany, Rwanda and Cambodia to daily cruelty to animals and children. But there are also sufficient examples of humans behaving decently towards each other to recognise this can be the basis for an ethic of being in the world.

That the world has sufficient resources and knowledge to ensure good life to everyone, and that the present division of wealth is obscene. The richest hundred people in the world could buy the gross national product of the poorest hundred countries (this is a guess, but almost certainly an accurate one). Nothing can justify this inequality, and in a world where a few people struggle to spend their money it is absurd that millions are hungry, living on the streets and without access to health and education.

That one of the factors perpetuating such inequality is an inability to imagine a commonality of human experience, a failure to recognise how our own wealth and happiness is bound up with others not suffering. At a daily level most of us would feel uneasy eating a sumptuous meal in front of a group of starving children. Yet once the connection is less obviously in front of us, we fail to make that connection. Political leaders, who like to invoke their religious faith, are conspicuously unable to translate Christ's teachings to do unto others as you would have others do unto you.

That to achieve a better world requires acknowledgement that we have more in common than not, irrespective of race, sex or country. For all the talk of recognising and respecting cultural differences, we should remember that all humans (and probably most animals) experience torture, hunger and death in remarkably similar ways. A poor Muslim woman in Bangladesh and a rich business man in Brisbane are indistinguishable in the face of bombs, earthquakes or famine.

That nationalism, whether secular or religious, is the greatest barrier to recognising this commonality. As the world seems both more integrated and more separate, divisions are increasingly justified in the name of religion and patriotism. Whole countries are branded as 'evil', and terror is defended in the name of love of God and country. If there is a lesson to be learnt from the nightly litanies of disaster on the television news it seems to be that reliance on religion is more likely to cause discord than harmony.

That to deny the props of belief in a supernatural being is to force us to believe in ourselves, and, therefore, to believe in others.

STELLA AXARLIS

Stella Axarlis has had five diverse professions – high school mathematics teacher, internationally acclaimed dramatic soprano, managing director of an engineering company, board member, and community advocate.

Among her many appointments she has been a member of the Prime Minister's Science Engineering and Innovation Council, the Victorian Premier's Economic, Environmental and Social Advisory Council, and Chair of Peninsula Health and Centre Health Interpreter Services Board.

Stella's current involvements include: Chair of the National Training Quality Council, Deputy Chair of the Australian National Training Authority Board, Chair of Liberti Learning, member of the Australian Universities' Quality Agency Board and the Phillip Island Nature Park Board.

In 1998 she became a Member of the Order of Australia for services to training, business, and children with special needs. She received a Hellenic Excellence Award in 2000, an Award for Excellence in Multicultural Affairs in 2002 and a Centenary Medal in 2003.

The tapestry of my life is interwoven with my strong beliefs in an Almighty Being; in people; in my origins; in Australia. I love this country and I'm passionately Australian.

I was born in Egypt and came to Australia with

my Greek parents and four brothers in 1950. My father was my greatest mentor in my earlier years and had a profound effect on me. He gave me the strength to break away from the mould even though he was very patriarchal.

My parents taught me to accept all creeds, all religions and all cultures, and to show respect and dignity towards our fellow human beings. This very strong foundation of Greek values is an integral part of my make-up.

Over four decades I have had five diverse professional lives and each of my careers has been crucial to my development as a human being. I think I have evolved very much along the way from my teaching, from my being an artist and performer, from my business leadership experience, and from my membership of boards.

A perfectionist, who pursues excellence in everything I do, I admit freely to being a workaholic. I could not possibly be without work. I embrace it and have always given 100 per cent, more in fact than was expected of me. I have always tried to be fair and maintain my sense of justice. I feel I have done my best and given everything I can. To judge myself is to know that I have contributed to the best of my ability.

My four passions are: that as a basic principle of democracy every Australian should have the right to a quality system of education and health; that we need to support Indigenous communities; that we need to fight for groups who do not have a voice; that we need to work towards becoming a truly equitable, multicultural and multiracial society.

As a nation we need to realise and understand there is so much we could do to support people who are disadvantaged, whether physically, intellectually, socially or economically.

We also need to try to understand and find a better way to support Indigenous communities. We need to work with the Indigenous leaders of each region to develop policies, strategies and actions that take into consideration the wisdom and local knowledge of their culture and people, rather than attempt to impose our policies.

I am a spiritual person and have evolved through my journey in a way that I'm comfortable with myself. It has been a journey with many twists and turns and I have been blessed with many opportunities. I believe it is still evolving and it has brought me to this stage in my life where I am content. But as for the future, I haven't a clue! There will be other challenges and even though I don't know what the next one will be, I'm sure it is just around the corner.

As I grow older, I often think of the Marschallin in the opera *Der Rosenkavalier* who tries to stop time flowing inexorably by stopping all the clocks. I am not afraid of time, because I enjoy growing older and in the process gaining a little wisdom. The older I get, the more courage I have to speak my mind, maintain my rebelliousness and challenge those who compromise and undermine an equitable society. I truly believe that one little voice can make a difference.

HELEN BARNACLE

Helen Barnacle is a psychologist with years of experience in drug and alcohol counselling. Now in private practice, Helen continues to work with drug-related offenders, victims of crime and the general community. Helen is also an artist and musician with years of experience performing and songwriting and in the last eight years has devoted considerable time and energy to utilising the arts to work with young people, particularly young women in custody in the juvenile justice system. Helen is also the author of *Don't Let Her See Me Cry*, an autobiography which tells her own story of heroin addiction and surviving the longest drug-related prison sentence ever meted out to a woman in Victoria.

I am now fifty years old, but I remember as a young person I lost my way. I recall looking at the world around me as a teenager and wondering, 'Where do I fit in?' I was at secondary school and my aim had been to be either a singer/musician or a physical education teacher. My two loves in life up to that stage had been calisthenics and music, particularly singing. I had been successful in both areas of my life although I was probably more passionate about singing.

However, on the inside things were starting to crumble and my confidence was waning. My home environment was deteriorating and where once I had felt loved and a sense of belonging, I now felt unloved, confused and unwanted. At the age of seventeen I left.

I searched the streets and found other unwanted, abused and neglected young adults – the rejects of society. Except that I didn't look down on them like most people did. I was fascinated by them: their strength and courage, their sense of humour. Girls working on the streets as prostitutes to pay for their next hit of heroin were in the sex industry because they didn't want to steal from people or burgle their houses. They didn't want to hurt others, but accepted the fact that they were often hurt, violated and assaulted. They became my friends. They should have been desolate, doing a job they hated, but they could still laugh. We all used heroin together and tried to pretend that everything was okay, but we were all running from something. The more we ran the more drugs we used and the drugs we used were illicit and so we ran into legal trouble. Most of us ended up in jail; many of my friends died before reaching the age of thirty.

While in jail and years into my very long sentence I found myself locked in an isolation cell, being punished further because I still hadn't found a way to stop wanting to use heroin. Searching again, I asked myself 'What does my life mean?' But I felt so worthless I didn't have enough strength left to find the answer, and because I didn't have an answer I just wanted to die. At the age of thirty I was all washed up. I thought to myself, 'It must at least be less painful to be dead . . .'

But, by this time, I had a four-year-old daughter. I couldn't let myself die because I desperately wanted to be her mother and although we couldn't be together for a few years, I knew the day would come when we would be reunited. How could I find a way to wait for that day without constantly being in pain? I searched my soul because to not find an answer this time meant to give up on life.

Eventually I found a way to feel peace inside and not have anguish in my heart. I would meditate daily, filling my heart with love and I'd send out compassion to others less fortunate than myself. Where self pity once lived, self belief started to grow and grow.

And now my grown up daughter is also my best friend. How lucky I am to have survived. How grateful I am to have found a way to believe in myself.

And now there's a new generation of young women and men working on the streets and using drugs. Now I'm not one of them, but I work with them. And in a way nothing has changed. They remain some of the most courageous people I have ever met.

In them I believe.

BEH KIM UN

Arriving in Australia from Penang, Malaysia in 1971 as a student, Beh Kim Un graduated in Applied Chemistry, majoring in colour. It was the exciting counter-culture and the political climate of seventies Carlton that led him away from industrial chemistry to the culinary world.

Since 1978, he has been actively involved in the food scene both locally and internationally. He is currently part owner of three diverse restaurants with his family and his lifetime partner, John Dunham. They are Shakahari (creative vegetarian), Isthmus of Kra (Nonya Thai) and Madam Fang (progressive Asian). Kim has extensively contributed recipes in Melbourne and overseas and collaborated with many notable chefs. Diane Horluigue, the former principal of The French Kitchen, is particularly inspiring. Having over twenty-five years of experience in the industry, his style reflects a strong and rich collage of multi-cultures. His current project is a collaboration with John Dunham to create a landscape sculpture farm in the Macedon Ranges.

It was in January 1997 that I literally experienced the common expression of 'here today, gone tomorrow'. Within a matter of fifteen minutes, rooms of ancient manuscripts, rare books, works of art and family history which my partner, John Dunham, and I had accumulated over twenty-five years were burned down and turned into a white sea of ashes.

I guess it is extremely rare to be a bushfire victim. It was surreal, eerie; a scene, I imagine, associated with the holocaust. Perversely though, it was precisely that moment which gave me an insight into life: life is so fragile. Somehow, it then made sense of the philosophy which I was brought up with, that is, living in the present, now.

I do not believe even for a moment, that any event which happens in life is accidental. With this intuition, I have followed my career path with great interest. One observation is that, although it has a certain rhythm and pattern, it has also constantly evolved and been reinvented. Thus I believe the only thing constant in life is change. I began my career as an industrial chemist specialising in colour. I then reinvented myself into a chef-owner managing three unique restaurants. At present, I am consumed with passion for incorporating the domain of landscape and garden design into the package of my life.

My fascination with colours began during my childhood years while growing up in a historic 1892 clubhouse in Penang, Malaysia. It had an enormous yet intriguing garden stacked with flora and fauna of the most vivid colours and century old gigantic tropical trees. The garden was especially mesmerising after the calm of the monsoon rain. Through the intensity of the reappearing sunlight, it never failed to reflect the magical qualities of the lively colours of nature. This was the realm of visual feast that directed me to the field of colour chemistry. However, later in life, I finally realised that the chemistry of organic colours is where my heart lies, and not the chemically produced ones.

My mother was an immensely creative and innovative chef with whatever local ingredients and utensils were available to her. She was like a magician, using food as her tool. She was constantly pushing boundaries by learning and absorbing knowledge from anyone who came her way. She endorsed the idea that the ultimate pleasure and happiness in cooking derives from satisfying all the five senses. Personally, my realisation of many years of trials and errors in commercial cooking is discovering the theory of taste equilibrium. This equilibrium is about harmonising the four tastes of hot, salty, sweet and sour to an optimal range which most of us can respond to naturally. Therefore, it is only to what point in this equilibrium range that makes each one of us vary in taste, which some of us defend and guard fiercely. Nonetheless, it is also by reaching this certain point that a chef becomes unique. This is what most chefs including myself work tirelessly for, the pursuit of this magical equilibrium point. In short, I believe this is my motivating life force in cooking.

Soon after the bushfire, John and I were searching for an ideal place to re-establish our lives. At first, we intended to rebuild in the same spot but eventually gave up on the idea. The cost of building a sensible, fireproof home in the most fire hazardous zone in the Dandenong Ranges was way too exorbitant.

Almost by accident, we stumbled across a property of 136 acres with an award-winning design house – our dream home! In fact, during the auction, I kept bidding with the thought that even if I have to work for the next twenty years to finance it, I will still go for it. I have no doubt that this is our destiny house as there was an instant connection. Our house is situated in a gentle valley with a three-kilometre river frontage teeming with wildlife. I believe we are in heaven! Six years later, we have created a space which interweaves the landscape with the works of many renowned sculptors.

Gardening has been my passionate love affair since childhood, although I am much more fanatical these days. Through gardening, I have discovered the meaning of ephemeral. Everything in a garden has a cycle. Behind the façade of a beautiful garden lies the anxiety, endurance, and sometimes disappointment, but mostly the creativity, of a gardener. Gardening is an unspoken language to dialogue and collaborate with nature. It has the power to humble our otherwise enormous egos. It is healing. It is life.

Landscaping is an act to embrace and to acknowledge the forms, space, time and elements in nature. In its most perfect design and moment, it reveals the wonder, which is life itself. In conclusion, I can comfortably say that the true meaning of my existence is to participate, to witness and to enjoy every moment it leads me to. After all, we are one and part of the Mystic Law!

ALAN BRISSENDEN

Alan Brissenden is a Shakespearean scholar who taught English at the University of Adelaide 1963–94. A dance critic since 1950, he was appointed a Member in the Order of Australia in 1996 for services to the arts. He has been married to Elizabeth since 1960, and they have three children and four grandsons.

When Dad was a teacher in the Riverina during the early 1930s, the Depression years, swaggies would knock on the school residence door ostensibly looking for a job – 'Any wood need chopping?' – but in reality often hungry for food. Mum used to make up packets of sandwiches and send them, grateful, on their way. From such early memories grew my belief that giving is good.

We later moved to a small bush school in the central west of New South Wales. It was in the bend of a creek, and birds were abundant. Long before words like 'environmentalist' entered common speech, Dad was teaching us principles of conservation. The foundations were being laid for my belief that ultimately we can never be owners of the land and its creatures; we are custodians, here for a brief time, with a God-given duty of care for them.

And despite the terrible things that we humans

have done and continue to do to the Earth, and to one another, I believe that humankind is fundamentally and mainly good – 'noble in reason . . . infinite in faculties . . . The beauty of the world, the paragon of animals', as Shakespeare has Hamlet say. When greed often seems to be the most powerful motivation for individuals, corporations and nations, it can be easy to fall into cynicism, sadness and despair. But generosity, hope and practical action are answers to the evil that men and women do.

Diagnosed with heart disease, I am protected and my life extended by an electronic implant and daily medication. How could I not believe that education and the development of knowledge are essential?

So, I believe in the future, and that it can be better than the past in an enormous number of ways. But we have to work at it, scientifically, imaginatively and creatively.

I believe in the healing power of beauty and the delight that it can give – the natural beauty of a waterfall, a soaring wedgetail eagle or a gurgling baby, the created beauty of art, music, dance or fine writing. Beauty can be stimulating, calming, exciting, relaxing. It can stir our guts, turn our thoughts in new directions, fill us with the joy of being alive.

Then there is prayer, which can take many different forms – I don't think you have to be especially religious to pray. There is so much to give thanks for, so many requests to make. Even though it may seem that prayers are not always answered, answers can come in unrecognised or unexpected ways.

My brother, Bob, and I were brought up Anglicans (Dad was a parish secretary, Mum a church organist). I left the church for more than a decade but was brought back to it again by my wonderful wife.

Finally, it comes down to love, however you define it. While I don't believe that all you need is love, as the Beatles' song has it, I do believe that love is a marvellous starting point, a pulsating springboard ready to launch us into life's next adventure, to explore new ways of giving, to take us into new realms of understanding, to bring us closer to people and to make the world a better place for those who come after us.

ELIZABETH BRODERICK

Liz Broderick is a partner with the law firm Blake Dawson Waldron. In the early eighties she recognised that technology would change business practices, and since that time has been instrumental in revolutionising the delivery of legal services both in Australia and internationally.

For many years Liz has been involved in the work/life balance debate and has written and presented widely on the subject. She has campaigned for workplace flexibility and has paved the way for other lawyers by becoming the first partner at her firm to work on a part-time basis. She also established Blake Dawson Waldron's social issues forum to assist in the development of a sense of community, not just for staff but for clients as well. She is on the Board of Blake Dawson Waldron and the Prince of Wales Medical Research Institute.

In 2001, she was Telstra's NSW Business Woman of the Year and also the 2001 Telstra Australian Business Woman of the Year in the Corporate Category. In 2003 she received a Centenary Medal for Service to Australian Society through Business Leadership.

Liz's story has been published in *The Ladies Room* and *What Women Want*, two books comprising a collection of stories about a diverse range of Australian women.

For My Father

When I asked my father what he would change if he had his life again, he said 'Nothing'. That surprised me. I hadn't expected it because he grew up in a typically impoverished Irish immigrant family, his parents died before he was ten, and he was touched by the horrors of World War Two.

But when I stopped and thought, I realised that without that adversity and experience, my father would never have become the wonderful teacher that he is. He would never have gained the wisdom to guide gently his children through the treasures and vicissitudes that form life's journey.

What follows is my father's views, his beliefs. And this is what he taught me.

On Happiness
Be positive and optimistic. Dare to be different and believe in yourself. If you adopt this approach to life, wherever you are, the sun will shine.

So much anxiety comes from the expectations that we place on ourselves, a feeling that we can't achieve the level that we believe others expect of us. Don't take on that burden.

On Intelligence
Someone once said 'Simple minds discuss people, average minds discuss events and great minds discuss

ideas'. It doesn't matter how simple the idea. It's the exploring that counts.

On Relationships

Life is a journey. It's important to make that journey with those you love because so much of the joy in life comes from personal relationships.

To build relationships you must be a good listener. That's so important. Listen first, and if you can bring together what you've heard in a way that's meaningful, teaches you a lesson or is amusing, well, that's a big bonus. Listening is the best way to understand someone else's experience.

Part of being a good listener is being open and perceptive. So many people just want a quick answer to a direct question and they want it now! They are content to skate on life's surface, not delving too deeply. If we're open to other people and we listen, who knows, we may get to travel to the most remarkable and unexpected places.

You've got to allow people to tell their story. You do this is by picking up on cues from their conversation and by responding. As a physician I used to spend my days listening to people tell their stories. Those stories were wonderful because they gave me insights into human existence that I couldn't have understood otherwise.

On Enjoyment

Enjoyment in life comes from simple things. I used to have so much fun as a child riding a horse very fast at night. I loved to speed through the blackness not knowing what was ahead or where I was going; the thrill was incredible. It is one of my fondest childhood memories and it taught me not to fear the unknown.

On Education

Education is very important. In poor families like mine, thankfully there was often someone who recognised the value of education and helped pursue it – usually the mother. Our mothers seemed to know instinctively that education was the way out of the cycle of poverty. But they also valued it for its own sake.

On Daily Life

Don't plan too far ahead. Always expect the unexpected – you can never know what life will throw at you. For example, getting married never occurred to me until the day I became engaged. If you had said to me 'What about getting married?', I would have said, 'I'm too young. That's for later on'.

But it's also important to let the dog see the rabbit. What I mean by that is, try to see from the outset the end point you are working towards. It will give you much more motivation.

On Stewardship
You need to know that there is something to hand down and I am not talking about monetary things. It's important to have a sense that you have contributed in some way to family, friends and others in their preparation for life. Believing you have done something that has made life easier and better for future generations – that's what life's all about.

These are my father's beliefs. These are my beliefs.

Dad, you have had enormous influence in my life.

Bob Carr

Bob Carr grew up in what is now his electorate of Maroubra, attending the University of New South Wales and working as a journalist at the ABC and *The Bulletin* before being elected to the New South Wales Parliament in 1983. In 1988 he was elected unopposed as Leader of the Opposition and in 1995 he became the thirteenth Labor Premier of New South Wales. He received the Fulbright Fiftieth Anniversary Distinguished Fellow Award in 2000. His best-selling collection, *Thoughtlines: Reflections of a Public Man*, was published by Penguin Books in 2002, and an extended essay, *What Australia Means to Me*, by Penguin in 2003.

I believe in reason. I put my faith in argument and commonsense. If the facts don't support my views I revise my views rather than ignore the facts. It follows that I distrust zealots, fanatics, dreamers, all those with single-issue agendas and simple solutions to complex problems. 'For every problem,' H. L. Mencken said, 'there is a neat, simple solution, and it is always wrong'. I believe the world is a better and safer place *because* it is complex: that there are checks to authority, and on every issue legitimate points of view, makes it harder for demagogues to impose their will. Complexity is one of the conditions – one of the safeguards – of our free, secular and pluralist society.

What I dislike about the conservative parties is not so much their respect for tradition (though this may be carried to excess, as it is on the republic), or their assumption that those of a certain class and background have a natural right to rule, but their complacency on issues of overwhelming concern: global warming, population levels, the future of the planet itself. I believe the first duty of a national government is to acknowledge the perils of greenhouse emissions and ratify the Kyoto protocols. The evidence of global warming, and the case for international action to reduce it, are incontrovertible; even if the case were not proved to everyone's satisfaction, the risks of disregarding the consensus of scientific opinion are too great to be countenanced. On this issue, no rational person will gamble.

Because I put my faith in reason, I want every one of our children to have the tools for rational discussion: literacy, numeracy, a sound education, a knowledge of history and our basic institutions. I see no reason why prosperity, survival and orderly economic growth should be dependent on a bigger population. The only result of a population of 50 million, such as many advocate for Australia, would be unsustainable and destructive over-development of our eastern coast – more freeways, more shopping malls, more cars, more petrol stations, more pollution, fewer rivers and forests and surviving species. Better a well educated population of 20 million than a population of 50 million with uneven educational standards inhabiting a concrete jungle.

In a humane and rational society we are bound to do everything possible to alleviate unnecessary suffering. One form of zealotry I especially dislike seeks to impede the progress of scientific and medical research. On the best advice available, medical science may soon have within its grasp the means to eliminate many of the cruellest and most intractable diseases. If embryonic stem-cell research can hold out hope for cures to degenerative diseases such as cancers, Alzheimer's, multiple sclerosis and other scourges I prefer to listen to those scientists who champion its use rather than those who oppose it.

Bertrand Russell called himself a 'cheerful pessimist'. I prefer to call myself a sceptical optimist. I believe we can move forward to a better life if we focus on the issues that count: safeguarding the planet, guaranteeing a better education for our young people, eliminating disease and suffering as best we can. We must content ourselves with a population level that the continent can sustain. If we do these things the other problems we face will be seen in clearer perspective. We will be better placed to tackle them with courage and clear thinking.

Kate Ceberano

Renowned for her soulful and powerful vocal style, Kate Ceberano has won almost every entertainment award in Australia. Kate first came to prominence as lead vocalist at seventeen years of age for the funk band, I'm Talking, and over the next twenty years went on to establish her highly successful solo career and a reputation as one of Australia's leading female singer/songwriters. Kate has released five Platinum albums and four Gold albums, which have sold in excess of one million albums in Australia alone, performed countless sellout tours, starred in acclaimed feature films and sell-out theatre productions, and hosted her own television show.

One definition for 'believe' in my *Websters New World* states, 'To have trust or confidence'.

It has been a great quest of mine to understand these two concepts and their interaction in my relationships with others, with my artistic endeavours and with ME. The last has been the most challenging.

As a child I was a dreamer, an optimist, a kid who wanted to love and be loved and who wanted others to love each other. It seemed I arrived with a pair of rose-coloured glasses perched firmly on my nose. They started to get fogged up around high school and by my early twenties had been well and truly sat on and left in cabs only to be returned to me by the good grace of some sad old driver who seemed to remember when he had 'a pair of glasses like that'.

Trust
The ability to trust oneself would be one of the highest virtues one could possess. Trust begins with having one's own moral code which, if violated, brings one down. The breakdown of integrity is the beginning of the end.

I had a weakness as a kid, which was that I changed my own point of view to make others right, offering myself up to their whims. This was to cause dire consequences in my later life and is perfectly explained in the word 'propitiation', which the dictionary defines as 'to appease'.

For example, I knew a guy who was an incredible artist who was also severely drug addicted. His friends said he was in control but I knew the drugs were controlling him, as they always do, but he managed to convince them all he was invincible. He wasn't. I did not have the courage at the time to stand up and disagree loudly when I was probably the only one he may have listened to. I was not a person to be trusted at that time.

A person you can trust will stand out from the crowd and say what they see, regardless of risk to comfort or status.

One can be untrustworthy to one's own art form

and sabotage it by allowing the opinions of others to change one's creativity because of money, or perhaps because the art has too much truth in it.

Trust of self requires self-discipline and love of self which has been earned.

Confidence

Belief in oneself is demonstrated by confidence, and the lack of it can create incompetence and inertia, crushing initiative and inspiration. At one time it was activity which preceded introspection. You found something you could do, you then did that and hopefully made a living out of it and that was that.

Today's culture has circumnavigated the psyche and come up with the idea that before one can act, one must 'feel' right about it. Thus we have a lot of people doing a lot of not a lot and 'thinking' too much!

Confidence comes from dreaming up something and having a go at it. You have to be wild, bigger than you are, braver, assume courage which does not come naturally, feign certainty and perhaps some of it will stick. And then just keep doing something and be willing to confront the consequences. While you may not get everything you set out to get, you will give out energy which will come back to you. Doing this has enabled me to live a fast, furious and fantastic life so far.

Greg Chappell

Greg Chappell played 87 test matches and captained Australia 48 times. He retired from test cricket as the highest run-getter in Australian test history (7,110) surpassing Sir Donald Bradman (6,996). He also set a new catching record for fieldsmen (122) and held the record for Australia for the most runs (380) scored in a test match. His total of four double centuries is second for Australia, behind Bradman, and he is the only Australian batsman since World War Two to have scored a century before lunch in a test. He is the only test captain to have achieved that feat.

He is the only Australian to score a century in each innings of a test on two occasions and the only test captain to make a century in each innings of his first test as captain. By scoring 182 in his last test innings Greg became the only test cricketer in history to score a century in his first and last test innings.

Greg was honoured by the Queen in 1979 with an MBE and was inducted into the Australian Sport Hall of Fame in December 1986. In December 2000 Greg was named in the Australian Test Team of the Century, in February 2002 he was inducted into the Australian Cricket Hall of Fame and in January 2003 was named Australia's fourth best cricketer ever behind Sir Donald Bradman, Shane Warne and Keith Miller. Greg was awarded an Australian Centenary Medal in May 2003.

The lessons I learned from the team sports I played have been invaluable to me in all aspects of my life. I grew up in a sporting family. Cricket, baseball and Australian football were our father's favourite sports so I was involved with all three from an early age.

Cricket was always going to be the main sport because Dad had a passion for the game. He soon inculcated that love in his three boys. Apart from playing, I watched, listened and read as much about the game and its heroes as I could. The big test matches of the era were those between Australia and England. I dreamed of one day representing Australia in an Ashes test series as I played my make believe test matches in the back yard.

I did not actually believe I would be good enough to play for my country. As one of the smallest boys in each class in primary school, and for the first few years of secondary school, I always struggled to match it with the bigger boys. Even though I eventually grew to a height of 188 cm I still don't think of myself as tall because of that early experience.

As I struggled with my size, and developed a huge inferiority complex because of it, I had to develop other survival techniques. Because we usually played on cement pitches that exaggerated the ball's bounce, I could not physically hit many balls. I had to learn to pick the balls I could and could not hit to score my runs. I also had to develop a few shots that the bigger boys did not need. It was a lesson in survival and creativity that proved invaluable later in my career.

Even as I grew and had success I could always identify other players who were much better than me. I was very nervous before games and sometimes found the pressure of waiting for my turn to bat almost overwhelming. Sometimes I almost wished myself out on reaching the wicket just to remove the 'sick feeling' in my stomach. I am sure I panicked myself into getting out on many occasions because of the pressure of wanting to do well to save personal embarrassment.

Despite all this self-sabotage I still managed to have some success along the way and steadily progressed through the grades. What I found was that the pressure increased rather than decreased as I made progress. There came an expectation, from others as well as myself, that I should keep scoring runs.

The lessons I learned through all this was that I got myself out more often than the opposition bowlers did. It was my mistake that usually led to my dismissal, rather than good bowling. Often some good bowling contributed to my mistake but in the end it was generally a mental error of mine that led to my dismissal.

One day it finally dawned on me that if I could take control of my state of mind I could change all of this. It didn't mean that I wasn't going to make mental errors but it did mean that I could delay the inevitable and bat for longer. I reckoned that if I batted for longer I must make more runs.

With that understanding I was able to relax and focus on the process of being successful rather than worry about the outcome. My mantra became 'Concentrate on the things you can influence and let the outcome take care of itself'.

SANTO CILAURO

While studying Law Arts at Melbourne University in the 1980s, Santo Cilauro performed in various comedy revues where he met Rob Sitch and Tom Gleisner. Teaming up with Rob and Tom, Santo wrote and performed for radio, and made his television debut as a member of The D-Generation in 1985. This collaboration later expanded to include Jane Kennedy and producer Michael Hirsh for the hugely success-ful *The D-Generation Breakfast Show* (Radio 3, Triple M) and in 1992, *The Late Show* (ABC TV).

Under the banner of Working Dog, Santo has continued to collaborate with Rob, Tom, Jane and Michael to create highly acclaimed film and television, including feature films: *The Dish* and *The Castle,* and television: *The Panel*, *All Aussie Adventures*, *Frontline*, *The Campaign*, *A River Somewhere*, *Funky Squad* and *The Late Show.* Publications include the first two books from the Jetlag Travel series: *Molvania – A Land Untouched By Modern Dentistry* and *Phaic Tan*, both published by Hardie Grant.

My grandfather believes you should never put all your eggs in the one basket. And he should know – every day during the War, he travelled from his tiny Sicilian village to the provincial capital where he sold eggs at the market. It was a bumpy three-hour trip on a crowded train through brigand territory.

If he put them all in one container he ran the risk of dropping, damaging, or even having the whole lot stolen. So he made sure he'd always leave some behind and those he did travel with he carried in various boxes. He decided that when there is a real danger of losing something, the most important thing is to make sure you don't lose *everything*.

I think in the western world we have become increasingly conditioned to 'back a winner'. For instance, I was asked the other day whether I believed in the Atkins Diet. I said, 'Sure, some of it.' I got a curious look back as if I was either 'Atkins' or 'The Zone'. The assumption was that there are only good choices and bad choices. Similarly, our adversarial system of law attempts to find a winner and a loser. When watching current affairs programs, we are presented with guys who wear white hats and those who wear black – as if we can't cope with anything in between.

Why? Because there is an assumption that we are all very busy and none of us have got much time. Choosing a winner is therefore a short-cut to finding the truth. But all of us know that in real life things are *never* black and white.

When it comes to beliefs, we are also pressured into putting our faith in 'one big thing'. However, if one day it doesn't bring the 'happiness' we thought it would bring, we risk feeling utterly lost and alone.

Which brings me back to my grandfather's eggs in their various baskets. Wisdom does not reside in one person, religion or philosophy. It lives everywhere and in everyone (with the possible exception of the person who wrote the 'Macarena'). I believe that in life, there is no one big answer – but many small ones.

Here's some stuff that over forty years of quiet observation I've either heard, read, deduced, intuited, made up, or just been confused by. None of the following is in itself groundbreaking – in fact, a lot of it is contradictory and some bits don't even make sense – but altogether, they give me a sense of balance.

The only two states of mind that are *never* productive are bitterness and complacency.

Our universal *goal* is to better ourselves as individuals, but our universal *desire* is to engage in meaningful communication.

Wealth should be measured not by what we carry on us, but what we carry *in* us. Our backgrounds and the stories that surround them are our riches. (Warning, the guy who told me that also believes the wrestling is real.)

The superfluous things in life are sometimes the most necessary.

'How is the world ruled and how do wars start? Diplomats tell lies to journalists and then believe what they read.' (Written in 1909, so I presume for 'diplomats' read 'politicians'.)

Now that I've started on quotes, let me hit you with my priceless collection of thoughts by Antoine-Marie-Roger de Saint-Exupery (the guy who wrote *The Little Prince*):

'Pure logic is the ruin of the spirit.'

'If you want to build a ship, don't drum up the

men to gather wood, divide the work and give orders. Instead, teach them to yearn for the vast and endless sea.'

'What makes the desert beautiful is that some-where it hides a well.'

That's where I'll stop with Saint-Ex. I particularly love that last one as I've always thought that the concept of 'unhappiness' is overrated. Unhappiness only exists because we know how wonderful it is to be happy. Conversely, happiness is wonderful only because we know the feeling is not permanent and therefore should be savoured before unhappiness inevitably returns. In a way, whether we're happy or unhappy is irrelevant – we will always oscillate from one to the other – the important thing is that we *feel alive* while we are either state. I'll put it more simply (and this is *so* Sicilian) – there is pain in pleasure and pleasure in pain and that is the beauty of life.

Right. I'm sure someone wise once said 'less is more' so that's it from me.

DIANE CILENTO

Diane Cilento was born and educated in Brisbane until the age of fifteen when she joined her family in the USA, where her father, Sir Raphael, worked for the World Health Organisation.

Her acting career began with a scholarship to the Royal Academy of Dramatic Art (RADA) in London. She signed a contract with British Lion and embarked on a series of films and plays in London and New York where she won a Tony, the Critic's Award, for *Tiger at the Gates* with Michael Redgrave in 1957. She married Sean Connery in 1962. Her films include *The Admirable Crichton*, *The Agony and the Ecstasy*, *The Wicker Man*, and *Tom Jones*, for which she was nominated for an Oscar as Best Supporting Actress (1964).

Diane returned to Australia in 1975 to play at the Queensland Theatre Company. The same year she bought 200 acres of rainforest in the Daintree and established Karnak with her then husband, the playwright Anthony Shaffer. In 1992 Karnak Playhouse was opened to the public, the vision of a 'theatre in the rainforest'. Since then it has been the home of many outstanding productions (*Ozopera* and *David Helfgott*). Anthony Shaffer passed away in 2001, not long after the world premier of his thriller, *The Thing in the Wheelchair*, directed by Diane at Karnak.

The theatre will be re-opened with a week-long festival entitled 'Romancing the Cane', a chronicling of three centuries of the sugar industry in North Queensland from 1888–2004 and beyond. The centrepiece will be a frank production of 'Doll 17' from Ray Lawler's *Summer of the Seventeenth Doll*.

Diane has written the books *The Manipulator* and *Hybrid*, and has just begun an autobiography.

Not long before Carl Gustav Jung's death, John Freeman inteviewed him for *Face to Face*. He asked the Swiss visionary if he believed in God.

There was a lengthy pause before a resounding 'No!' hit the airwaves and hung there like an unexploded grenade. A rather flustered Freeman tried to reorganise his next question. Before he could do so, Jung's rasping voice was heard again and the camera quickly cut back to him.

'I do not haff to believe . . . I *know*!'

From the first 'No' to the second 'know' we could feel the enormity and passion of Jung's journey . . . the doubts, fear, pain, isolation and final certitude that had brought him to that place. There was no need to say any more. It was an unforgettable moment.

'Believe' seems to be an untrustworthy word, perhaps because it has 'lie' embedded in its heart.

Today there are more media sceptics, like me, than ever before. We have been led to believe so many lies by spin doctors and politicians that we have become shy of giving full credence to anything we read in the press or hear on TV.

The first sentence in *The Kernel of the Kernel*,

written in the 13th Century by the Sufi sage Muhayiddin ibn Arabi, reads: 'Now know this . . . A person of knowledge never fixes his belief in any one form.'

Throughout history fixed beliefs have caused havoc and death to literally billions of people. The slave trade could never have flourished if the white man had not embraced the ludicrous but rigidly held belief that all black men had smaller brains, were therefore inferior and only fit to be their slaves. The Inquisition, where thousands were tortured to death for not conforming to the beliefs of the church hierarchy; the Holocaust, Apartheid, the massacres in Rwanda and Kosovo, as well as the recent invasion of Iraq . . . in short, persecution of anyone who does not adhere to the particular form of one belief . . . this is the legacy of fixed 'beliefs'.

I think it is very healthy to be a non-believer, one who does not make snap judgements that set like cement in our souls; one who looks with impartiality, who prods and probes until what is left is the truth. It is also incredibly difficult to hold out against friends and family who urge one to believe what they do, who cannot understand that you can't see what seems obvious to them. From family feuds to civil war, it is said that interior rifts are the bitterest of all.

'Seeing is believing' has lost its meaning since special effects and virtual reality were invented, and our 'big toys' have become so overpowering in their ability to blow up the world, fly to Mars, spy on anybody on the planet, or decimate populations with deadly gases. The greatest fear must be that these awesome weapons come into the hands of men of fixed beliefs, who feel justified in using them to condone their acts.

I lie in bed and set my mind free from all these horrors to soar through space and time like winged Pegasus.

My mind and the instruments of hearing, sight, smell, touch, taste and imagination connect me with the wealth of possibilities that man's ingenuity has produced . . . to relish exquisite paintings, sculptures, installations and architecture, to savour music whether classic, ethnic, hip-hop or jazz, to appreciate and even participate in dance, see dramas from Shakespeare to Stoppard, read myriad collections of books, surf the Internet, watch docos on TV.

The privilege of being alive today is to be part of the massive ongoing creative outpouring that is available should we so choose.

This I *do* believe.

PETER COSGROVE

General Peter Cosgrove, AC, MC, Chief of the Defence Force since 2002, has the military life in his blood. Perhaps best known for his role as Commander of the International Forces in East Timor (INTERFET) in 1999 and Australian of the Year in 2001, Peter has served in the military for almost forty years.

He attributes much of his success to his family, in particular his wife Lynne and their three sons. Peter is a passionate rugby supporter, owns a set of golf clubs and enjoys the occasional game of cricket.

It's not good to start such a treatise with a whinge, but I can't help myself! Just like all of you, I'm incredibly involved with day-to-day life. I suppose I very rarely stop to think about what I am or even who I am in the sense that our beliefs and values closely define that identity. So, to be asked to take a breath, to reflect and describe life's essence was difficult, even intimidating when life continues to lie in wait, to be lived, enjoyed, savoured, sometimes survived, but is always, always so demanding. So, courage, Cosgrove, and get on with it (so much of my present writing is in the spare, bureaucratic style of my calling that my values might be listed as a half-dozen single-word dot points)!

From where do our beliefs spring? Do they come with us from our mother's womb – are they inherent? Or are they inculcated by our upbringing? Are some of them a universal part of the human psyche? I really don't know but I'm sure that throughout our lives our beliefs are educated and honed and given focus and voice by our experiences – not made empirically better or comparatively superior, just given form and clarity.

It's hard to rank beliefs but perhaps there are some at the core of truly good and thus truly great people. I believe that above all we must have a tolerance, a sense of compassion, of empathy, a generosity of spirit which guides and governs all our relationships with others of our community, from our family to the global community. Not an unquestioning or unrequited sentiment, for it is one that should earn and receive respect, but what we Australians cryptically and inevitably refer to as 'a fair go'. I thus believe in a 'fair go' for all. We will give the shirt off our backs to those less fortunate but we do not like to be taken for a ride.

I believe profoundly in trust. Trusting human nature and trusting people is for me an automatic choice. Of course experience tells me that this is frequently and endlessly conducive to disappointment, but the corollary is worse: to go through life distrustful is so stunting, so limiting on our short time of life's grace that I'm prepared to wear the odd let-down. Those who know my calling may find this strange, but trust is not blind and can be suspended for professional purposes!

I believe in the fundamental responsibility we have for each other, starting with our family and extending endlessly outwards. To make sense of our time on earth we need to have a fundamental purpose and that must be to enable ourselves, but even more so our kids, to live life peacefully, healthily, enjoyably and productively, all the days of our lives. To this end, an anonymous Dad and Mum in any suburb, striving their all for their kids, may therefore look presidents and billionaires in the eye and not as inferiors!

This sense of responsibility, indeed accountability for each other, this need to protect and nurture the present and future human condition, leads me to my final belief in this brief sermon. There are some challenges and affronts which cannot be countenanced and which must be prevented or redressed – not casually or joyfully, not without risk or damage to the human spirit, but for the greater good. In recognition, nations grudgingly give up the treasure of their youth to their armed forces. Presently, I command this part of Australia's national treasure. I believe in them.

TIM COSTELLO

Reverend Tim Costello is currently the Chief Executive at World Vision, Australia. He came to that role in 2004 after many years as a Baptist Minister in inner-city Melbourne where he focussed on issues of social justice ranging from fair gambling to homelessness and substance abuse. He created a not-for-profit organisation called Urban Seed. Prior to that he worked as a lawyer mainly dealing with family and criminal law.

Tim is well-known throughout Australia as a passionate speaker and motivator. He lives in Melbourne with his wife Merridie and three young adult children.

I very rarely get asked the question as to what I believe. Maybe as one known by the tag 'Reverend' people think it is pretty obvious. You know, he must believe all that churchy stuff, whatever that is. But my suspicion is that very few people ask others what they believe, no matter what tag they wear. It just isn't seen as being of enormous import. So long as one is a 'good bloke', can enjoy a few jokes and knows what is going on with the AFL, not much else really matters.

But it is true that throughout history people have been prepared to give their life for their beliefs. As a child I read many missionary biographies, which inspired me because of the courage of exceptional men and women who went to all sorts of remote corners of the world to take the gospel of Christ to those who otherwise would never have heard of it. I remember feeling awe at thinking of them in the face of cannibals, witch doctors and long, lonely separations from all their loved ones. And then there were the heroic examples of martyrs like Dietrich Bonhoeffer, who took a carefully thought out theological stand against the Third Reich and, despite being a pacifist, participated in the plot to kill Hitler. At thirty-nine he was to pay for this with his life, executed by Hitler just seven weeks before the end of World War Two.

So when I think about what I believe the question comes to mind as to what ultimately matters to me and gives me passion and courage to live.

I know I believe that life is a wonderful gift and it is worth living each moment as fully as one is able. I sense in my bones the goodness of life. As I walk near the surf, or run in a beautiful autumn garden I see the beauty of nature and just find myself saying a deep-seated 'thank-you'.

I know I believe that there is more to life than just the material things around us. I believe in the importance of the spirit as a guiding force in life and those things that kill the spirit need to be named and opposed. This is one reason why I have put energy over the last ten years into the gambling debate. I see the greedy, sinister forces at work behind the gambling industry as crushing the spirit and the will of many vulnerable people.

I know I identify in the person of Jesus Christ a unique spiritual force. I believe he is more than just a man. To me he is the word of resistance God has spoken into our world. I find his life so inspiring and his death and resurrection overwhelmingly redemptive. I know that I am compelled to be part of those who identify that their lives are aligned to him and the 'kingdom of God' that he proclaimed.

Finally I know I believe in justice. In my position with World Vision I get to travel to many parts of the world and I am aware more than ever of the inequalities and the excessive greed and corruption of power that is feeding this injustice. I know I cannot sit back and not be part of action to change the attitudes and behaviours that entrench de-humanisation and poverty.

Ultimately I think beliefs are best judged by the way a person lives their life. Jesus said 'By their fruits you shall know them.' I think that sums it up and is certainly the creed I seek to live out and the criteria by which I make assessments of other people.

BRYCE COURTENAY

Bryce Courtenay, AM, was born in South Africa and educated in Johannesburg and the UK. He arrived in Australia in 1958 and became an Australian citizen the following year.

He entered the advertising industry, and over a career spanning thirty-four years was the Creative Director of McCann Erickson, J Walter Thompson and George Patterson Advertising. During this period he was much awarded, both in Australia and overseas.

As a speaker he was invited by the Chinese Government to give the first series of lectures on the subject of advertising and free enterprise. He has lectured on the power of the individual to achieve any end purpose in Asia, the UK, the USA, New Zealand, South Africa, Canada and in his own country, and is rated as one of the top five speakers in Australia.

However, he is best known as Australia's top selling-novelist with titles such as *The Power of One*, which is translated into eleven languages and the subject of a major movie of the same name, *Tandia*, *April Fool's Day*, *The Potato Factory*, *Tommo and Hawk*, *The Family Frying Pan*, *A Recipe for Dreaming*, *The Night Country*, *Jessica*, *Solomon's Song*, *Smoky Joe's Café*, *Four Fires* and *Matthew Flinders' Cat*. His newest work, *Brother Fish*, will be published in November 2004.

In 1995 Bryce Courtenay was awarded the Order of Australia.

We are told that our belief systems are usually inculcated in childhood, some negative, others positive, so
that parents and institutions – religious and others –
are responsible for what we come to believe as adults.
The influences on my young life were a mixture of
all of these. I was born illegitimately, or to use the
common euphemism, to a single parent. This involved
some time spent in an orphanage and some with
a mother prone to nervous breakdowns, who had
embraced a charismatic religion. Finally at the age of
eleven, I received a scholarship to a boys school closely
patterned on the English public school system.

Putting all this together as the bunch of influences
that formed my character, it may be said that I was
lonely, frequently bullied, often whipped, trusted few
adults, and soon realised that institutions regarded
anyone who appeared to be an individual or clever
with great suspicion; sadness was a common emotion. Furthermore, I knew at an early age that I was
a sinner and therefore filled with guilt and would
need to be saved by being born again. To round
things off, I was influenced by the teachings of a
bigoted, supposed racially superior, white male
supremacist, upper-class South African boys' boarding school. Taking all these things into consideration
there seemed little room for a positive belief system
to emerge.

However, my first belief is that we are responsible for ourselves. A teacher once informed me
that the best helping hands you are ever likely to
experience are attached to your wrists. I became a

very competent boxer so that any bigger boy taking me on soon knew I was no pushover. I was said to be very bright, but I think it was more that I refused to give up; in the end it was persistence more than anything that won the day. I decided that between the Dutch Reformed Church (orphanage), the Apostolic Faith Mission (parent) and the Church of England (boarding school) it was probably a good idea to fashion my own sense of God – someone who expects me to exercise the more noble aspects of humanity and who doesn't wish to be constantly bothered with the things in life I ought to be able to take care of myself.

This was all very well, but it didn't quite take care of my low self-esteem, an almost inevitable result of the childhood I had lived. I decided to hide this sense of inadequacy, and there are two places where a child can safely do this. The first is to merge with the crowd, to become nothing in particular, neither noticed or noted. Dead average is always a safe hiding place. The second is way up front, the 'catch me if you can' position. And so I tried my best to excel, to use to the full extent what small gifts I had been given. In the process I developed a mantra for my life which goes like this:

When you're skating on thin ice, you may as well tap dance.

I also think of it as 'the power of one', that ability we all have to overcome the negative influences in our lives and to finally triumph without having to become a bastard; to spit in the face of adversity and circumstance and to refuse to be beaten by either or both.

These days spontaneous kindness is looked upon as a need to be loved by everyone; charity is seen as a manifestation of guilt; happiness is regarded as a lack of intelligence and even pity has to be carefully qualified to receive the approbation of one's peer group. At the age of six I recall being made to learn, by shouting out by rote, what my kindergarten teacher at the time termed 'Our very nice saying':

> I shall pass through this world but once,
> any good thing I can do, or any kindness
>   I can show
> to any fellow human being . . . let me do it now,
> for I shall not pass this way again.

It hardly seems appropriate in today's cynical world, but after all the effort I've put into life, I have come to the conclusion that 'Our very nice saying' is what I believe life is intrinsically all about.

SUE DENGATE

Sue Dengate is a psychology graduate and former high school teacher. As a result of her own children's experiences she became a food intolerance counsellor with an interest in the effects of foods on children's behaviour, learning and health. Her *Fed Up* series of books are bestsellers and her research into the behavioural effects of a common bread preservative has been published in a medical journal. She and her husband, a food technologist and former research scientist, run the Food Intolerance Network.

In the 1970s I trekked more than 2000 km in Nepal, exploring the mountains and learning about the people and religions in that fascinating country. I was particularly attracted to the Buddhist idea of the middle path between asceticism and excessive self-indulgence. Guidelines for achieving this included right mindfulness, right speech and right livelihood, or earning one's living in a way that is not harmful to others.

I also admired the work of Mahatma Gandhi, the charismatic Indian lawyer who successfully advocated non-violence as a method of defeating the British in India. Although he was writing in the first half of the twentieth century, some of Gandhi's ideas seem even more relevant now, particularly when he deplored 'science without humanity' and 'commerce without morality'.

At that time, I could never have foreseen the path my life would take. After I had my first baby, I was overwhelmed by the turmoil of a child whose behaviour and sleep patterns were disrupted by food additives. The more I found out about food chemicals, the more amazed I became that the changes I could see with my own eyes could be ignored or denied by the government, doctors and the food industry. In what was to become my life's work, I started researching, writing and speaking about this issue and helping thousands of other families in the same position.

I found that certain food chemicals can destroy health or family harmony and prevent students from reaching their potential, perhaps for the rest of their lives, yet most people who are affected are completely unaware, as I had been, of why this is happening.

In my work, I encounter plenty of people with livelihoods that harm others, from the fast food industry, to bakers using preservatives in their bread, to regulators who are supposed to be protecting consumers. They always claim that only a few are affected, as if that makes it all right to knowingly harm others. There is also Gandhi's 'science without humanity' in the form of food industry funded studies that find or report only what the funding bodies want to hear. And then there is 'commerce without morality'. Billions of advertising dollars are spent by corporations seeking to increase profits by selling products that contribute to obesity, ill health and behaviour problems. The self indulgence and materialism they promote are inimical to health and happiness, and the words of Gandhi seem more important than ever: 'Do not be drawn away from the simplicity of your ancestors'.

My children are grown up now and have left home. They have benefited from my work, but I continue to do it because I believe that I can change the system to prevent harm to other children. Every day I receive emails of thanks from grateful parents.

I believe there is a very delicate balance in nature and when we interfere, we risk unintended consequences. I work at the small end of the scale, helping troubled families with kids affected by food chemicals. But what I see is a microcosm for our planet with its widespread disruption and extinctions, deforestation, and climate change due to technological overkill. Like the Lady Galadriel in *Lord of the Rings*, I believe that even the smallest person can make a difference.

JOHN DOWD

The Honourable Justice John Dowd, AO, was a judge of the Supreme Court from 1994 to 2004, and is Queen's Counsel in NSW and the ACT. He is also admitted in Papua New Guinea and Ireland, and is Chancellor of Southern Cross University.

In 1975 he was Member for Lane Cove in the NSW Parliament, and was Leader of the Opposition from 1981 to 1983. From 1989 to 1991 he was Attorney-General and Leader of the House, and from 1992 to 1994 was Consul-General from the Cook Islands to Australia.

Justice Dowd is President of the Australian Section, International Commission of Jurists (ICJ); International Commissioner of the ICJ; and Chairperson of the ICJ Executive Committee in Geneva.

One has only to contemplate a newly born child with its infinite individuality, from fingerprints to almost every individualised part of its anatomy, to understand the marvellous entity which is the human being, with incredible potential for self-fulfilment and creativity.

The human being is by nature, however, a social animal, and thus society must work out rules of courtesy and accommodation, in order to live in a collective society. From before a child has even acquired reason, societies endeavour to create rules restricting individuality, requiring conformity. This is governed by social and religious customs, conventions, and the law.

I was born at the beginning of World War Two. I found at an early age that girls were treated differently, then, as the war progressed, I became aware that there were these different people, such as Germans and Japanese, who were called 'enemies'. Next I realised that there were more different people, called 'Baptists' and 'Catholics', and then another group, called 'Asians'.

Later I learned there were people called 'migrants', who looked and spoke a little differently. Eventually, to my childhood despair, I discovered that there were people in other parts of the world whose lives were totally repressed. There were societies which saw it as a duty to prevent women, in particular, from rising out of the repression created by the rules and customs of those societies. Next I discovered that there were other people who were different, called 'homosexuals'.

I had made the mistake, perhaps, of being always in the majority, but soon began to realise, as a result of my early Christian training, that these people whom I had been taught were equal in every way, were far from equal, and I saw it as my duty to do what I could to remove inequality wherever I found it.

The difficulty of a democracy, which is the preferred form of government to any other, is that by its very nature it governs by majority. So too does public opinion work by majority, particularly through the influence of the mass media.

Those who are unpopular, or in a minority, or guilty of crimes, have difficulty obtaining access to the law and having their views recognised by parliaments and public opinion.

When the majority feels insecure and fearful, there is a tendency for its members to protect themselves by supporting legislation which ignores individual human rights and principles of natural justice.

The difficulty of every society is in balancing the needs of the majority and the needs of the minority, particularly in times of stress or adversity. It is a moral duty to speak out in defence of the unpopular and oppressed, so that society is encouraged to accommodate within its broad aims the needs and rights of individuals and the entitlement of everyone, including that new-born babe, to fulfil his or her potential.

We should work to ensure that, not only in our society but in other societies, the oppressed have their entitlements fulfilled. Our endeavours should be not just for those who are powerful, or for those who are popular, or for those who come from more affluent and educated societies.

It is the nature of the press and of politicians to emphasise the need for a society to protect itself, and to justify repression of individuals rather than take individual needs into account. Good legislation balances individual needs with majority rights. We must not sacrifice the rule of law, and the protections we have built up, to the need of governments to be seen to be doing something about a problem.

The duty of an individual to speak out in favour of minority rights does not arise from the need of that individual or the minority, but from the need of society itself. A society which does not look after individual human rights does not look after itself.

NICK EARLS

Nick Earls is the author of ten books, including the bestselling novels *Zigzag Street*, *Bachelor Kisses* and *Perfect Skin*. His work has been published internationally in English and also in translation, and this led to him being a finalist in the Premier of Queensland's Awards for Export Achievement in 1999.

Zigzag Street won a Betty Trask Award in the UK in 1998, and is currently being developed into a feature film. *Bachelor Kisses* was one of *Who Weekly*'s Books of the Year in 1998, and is currently being adapted for television.

He has written three novels featuring teenage central characters, and *48 Shades of Brown* was awarded Book of the Year (older readers) by the Children's Book Council in 2000. His earlier young-adult novel, *After January*, was also an award-winner. Both have been successfully adapted for theatre.

The Thompson Gunner, a breakthrough novel for Earls, was published in August 2004.

Nick Earls is the chair of the Australian arm of the international aid agency War Child. He is also patron of Kids Who Make a Difference and an honorary ambassador for both the Mater Hospitals Trust and the Abused Child Trust in Queensland.

His contribution to writing in Queensland led to him being awarded the Queensland Writers Centre's inaugural Johnno award in 2001 and a Centenary Medal in 2003.

He has an honours degree in Medicine from the University of Queensland, and lives in Brisbane. London's *Mirror* newspaper has called him 'the first Aussie to make me laugh out loud since Jason Donovan'.

I believe in maintaining a questioning mind and, whenever possible, giving it the time to ask the questions it needs to ask. I believe in maintaining a willingness to give due consideration to another's point of view, and in trying to remember that willingness in the moments when it's tested.

I believe that dogma stands up poorly when it meets the fullest version of the facts, and that almost nothing can be reduced to the convenience of a sound bite. I believe that too many of our views are based on assumptions, inaccuracies and fractions of the true story, but that those are sometimes the best information we are given and we should remember that each time we form a view.

I don't believe in taking action without due regard to consequences, but I also believe it is usually better to do the best we can at the time than do nothing. I believe in trying not to make the same mistake twice. I believe in picking my battles, and in choosing an option other than battle whenever it's open to me.

I don't believe in prioritising the short term over the long term.

I believe that many rules have exceptions – rules are simple, and circumstances tend not to be. I believe we should expect to have to manage contradictions and inconsistencies.

I believe in balance and fair negotiation.

I believe in compassion and tolerance, though I know that tolerance is easy in principle and intolerance is easy to recognise in others.

I believe in working to develop a measure of selflessness and that, when the focus is on us, we can sometimes turn it somewhere else where it will do more good. I believe in the use of a position of privilege to benefit those who are less privileged. I believe in charity over indifference, and empowerment over charity. I believe that treating everyone fairly does not necessarily mean treating everyone the same.

I believe in careful food handling and the importance of clean water. I believe in vaccination. I don't believe in most common cold remedies, or other treatments based on no more evidence than a rumour heard twice. I believe in scientific method, and that randomised double-blind trials are the best way to decide what works and what doesn't.

I believe in learning from recipes, though not necessarily following them.

I believe in the separation of the church and state, the separation of parliament and the judiciary, and the presumption of innocence. I don't believe borders are as important as we're sometimes told.

I believe in the pursuit of happiness, the company of friends and in making the most of straightforward things (mangoes, waves, mountains, mini-golf).

I don't believe in tidiness, nor in fashion.

I believe that our common humanity must

ultimately count for more than the ways in which we differ from each other, even across great distances.

Hazel Edwards

Amongst Hazel's 150 books, one in particular, *There's a Hippopotamus on our Roof Eating Cake* (which is now twenty-five), has been read by millions of children. *Hand Me Down Hippo* (Penguin) is its new, mini, female cousin, illustrated by Mini Goss.

After the 2001 Australian Antarctic Division expedition to Casey Base, Hazel wrote *Antarctic Writer On Ice*, an eco-thriller, *Antarctica's Frozen Chosen*, and a picture book, *My Dad's Gone to Antarctica*. She is currently involved in *Hot Ice Squad*, a pre-school TV animation/toys series based on Antarctic vehicles.

Hazel is also interested in ideas crossing media; her adolescent *Fake ID* is being televised, and genealogists use her *Writing a Non Boring Family History*.

Hazel is married with two adult children, and a five-year-old grandson for whom she writes a story each birthday.

I never thought I'd be belly dancing in Antarctica.

Luckily, I had an unconventional father. He believed that it was okay to be different as long as it wasn't used as an excuse to avoid hard work. That was my legacy of belief. Very useful for an author who often needs to have the viewpoint of an outsider.

Listen. Ask questions if you don't understand.

Respect others' culture even if you don't believe in their religion or politics. Treat everybody equally, whether millionaire or drop-out, until they give you reason to do otherwise. My father believed in the Socratic method of asking questions until the replier found their own solution.

As an author I've been grateful for my father's legacy, despite his early death when I was twenty-four. Even though my husband and I are agnostics, and not Jewish, we sent our children to a Jewish school where learning is valued. They've had the experience of being outsiders which has led to mutual tolerance and respect.

Creativity is a survival skill, like a sense of humour, and one that isn't tested on the preliminary Antarctic medical.

Two years ago, on an Antarctic expedition, I was stuck in the ice on a beset polar ship with thirty-four men and three other women expeditioners. Either it could be seen as adventurous research, to be confined with Antarctic experts on elephant seals, glaciology and polar medicine, or as a sentence with no release date.

Creative problem solving is a matter of putting together two things which have not been in that combination before. So I started the first Antarctic belly dancing class for female expeditioners. It was really an anti-boredom exercise to music to get us up in the morning. I kept interviewing the beset expeditioners about their work styles and wrote a children's story about icebergs – *Lachieberg* – which each e-mailed to their children after find-and-replacing their child's name to personalise the story.

Words matter, especially as a way of coming to terms with extreme experiences. Creativity, technology and business are not in conflict, but are complementary. And a goal is a dream with a deadline. To influence reality, dreams must be structured and shared in a format others can understand.

Often a creator must judge 'success' by internal criteria, the gap between aspiration and the creation. The journey you choose may follow a different route from others, so it is unfair to judge 'success' or 'failure' by criteria to which the creator did not aspire.

I knew that writers didn't earn much. But I wanted a varied work style that would be mentally stimulating and people-centred. So I am grateful for an enriched life where I have interviewed ice-pilots, belly dancers and geneticists and have been a participant-observer from Nepal to New Zealand. My family has benefited from meeting puppeteers, cartographers, trekkers and musicians.

Authors are often asked challenging questions.

'Do you have any other books I can read like *There's a Hippopotamus on Our Roof Eating Cake*?'

She was the mother of a five-year-old prep student in a remote school. As an author I had been talking with parents about encouraging their children to read. She was about thirty, neatly dressed, and waited until the other parents had finished. She said nervously, 'It's the only book I have ever read. Those words have patterns I can work out. My daughter is in prep and is learning to read. I'm learning with her.'

What courage. Admitting illiteracy, especially near other parents.

That incident was a significant reminder to me. An idea can have the power to move and influence, but the skills to shape those words are also important.

And some questions require courage to ask and must be answered.

Once a book is published, it has a life of its own. It may go places I have never been, it is a book-child out on its own. An embryonic idea that has walked.

Like the African saying, 'Have patience, in time even an egg will walk.'

RON ELISHA

Ron Elisha was born in Jerusalem in 1951 and migrated with his family to Melbourne in 1953. He graduated in Medicine from Melbourne University in 1975 and began writing for the stage in 1977. His stage plays include *In Duty Bound* (1979), *Einstein* (1981), *Two* (1983), *Pax Americana* (1984), *The Levine Comedy* (1986), *Safe House* (1989), *Esterhaz* (1990), *Impropriety* (1993), *Choice* (1994), *Unknown Soldier* (1996), *The Goldberg Variations* (2000) and *A Tree, Falling* (2003). He has also written a telemovie, *Death Duties* (1991), two children's books, *Pigtales* (1994) and *Too Big* (1997), and feature articles in a variety of publications.

The universal backdrop to life is fear.

The specifics of that fear vary from one culture to the next, from one individual to the next, but one thing is clear: Life is pretty scary.

In order to cope with that fear – whether it be the fear of spiders, or of public speaking or of death – we create for ourselves the illusion of control. The illusion, in other words, that what we do influences in some predictable way what happens to us.

One of the central means by which we attempt to exercise this control is by naming things. Nomenclature confers a sense of understanding of the named entity, from which we derive the comfort of potentially being able to act upon that understanding.

Prolonged lethargy, then, becomes Chronic Fatigue Syndrome, within which term (though essentially meaningless) lies the implicit promise of symptom relief and cure.

A chaotic, unjust and ultimately unfathomable world takes on manageable proportions if we interpret its perversity in the light of a presence we like to call God. If all of the shit that happens is under the control of a single Being, and we have access to that Being, then we have access to that control.

As a youngster, I accepted God as a fair if uncomfortably wrathful given. With the acquisition of knowledge, experience and a little common sense, the notion of an omnipotent presence grew at first faintly and then overwhelmingly ridiculous.

The power vacuum created by the demise of the Supreme Being cried out for an alternative understanding of the way in which the world might work. Myriad philosophies each held out the vaguely patronising hand of hope, each hope successively dissolving as the words which formed its vessel were dissected to the point of sound and fury, signifying nothing.

Politics had already proven itself manifestly corrupt, and drugs, though admirably palliative in the short term, held out no new insights and a freedom as illusory as it was enslaving.

With the advent of the 'Me' generation, we were asked to believe in ourselves. Understand yourself and the world is your oyster. Have faith in yourself, and you can achieve anything you set out to achieve. You are the master of your own fate.

But the world was never anyone's oyster. And no-one really understands anything, least of all themselves. Added to which, how can one have faith in something that was crippled long before it was able to defend itself? The fact is that fate, by virtue of its non-existence, has no master at all.

Then, of course, we realised our mistake. Me is nothing without Us. We live only through and within the consciousness of those we touch. The love of others and our love for them is what truly makes it possible to take on the world.

But is that what the Ultimate Truth of the universe boils down to? Safety in numbers? Surely, if history has taught us anything, it is that within numbers there resides anything but safety.

Perhaps the inadequacy of all of these solutions rests with the very notion of a belief or a creed in itself. Perhaps we would do better to eschew such ephemeral and ill-conceived goals altogether, simply accepting the world for what it is: Chaotic, unjust and heinously scary.

JOHN ELLICE-FLINT

John Ellice-Flint was born in Sydney in 1951 and spent his childhood on a sugar cane farm in northern New South Wales.

Early in life John developed a love of nature and studied geology at the University of New England in Armidale, eventually pursuing a career in an industry that kept him in touch with the natural environment.

At age twenty-two, John left Australia to work for a multinational oil and gas company and returned to Australia twenty-six years later to head up the Australian oil and gas company, Santos Limited.

During his time abroad, he lived and worked in many different countries, including Japan, Singapore, Indonesia, Holland, Norway, the UK, the United States, Russia, Azerbaijan, Syria and Yemen.

I have been fortunate in my life to have lived and worked in many countries and experienced the diversity and richness of many different cultures. This has certainly shaped the way I view the world.

After agreeing to contribute to this book there were two distinct but related themes that came to mind as I started to focus on what my response would be.

Firstly, I realised how much my own life has been

enriched by my experience of other places. I believe that for Australia, as an island continent, opening ourselves up to the rest of the world presents us, not only with an enormous challenge because of distance, but with many opportunities.

We are a nation of great explorers and we should actively encourage our young people to explore the world in the hope that they return to Australia with ideas that are positively influenced by the knowledge they gain from these new experiences and different cultures.

The desire to seek new experiences is often initiated during our formal education. If our education system can foster a desire for life-long learning then we are more likely to want to seek new experiences and ideas to feed the brain. When I was fourteen years old I had a science teacher, Allan Cameron, who made science and the natural world, particularly geology, come alive for me and I will never forget this experience.

I believe we need to raise the bar in education. This means encouraging our young people both to stay at school longer and to pursue their interests at a tertiary level, and that also means participating in the training programs that develop the specialist manual skills that we need.

Australia, along with the rest of the planet, faces many challenges in terms of managing its natural resources so that we balance our present needs with those of the future.

How we manage these natural resources – such as

energy and water – is necessarily of great concern to the entire Australian population.

We need to rethink the way we use our scarce resources so that Australia makes the most of what it has. What should we be encouraging in terms of alternative energy? The solutions we find will be a mix of policy and ideas and every individual will have to think differently about the way we use energy and water. At a personal level, we need to do what we can to make our homes more energy and water efficient. Industry needs to design products and systems that support our endeavours. For instance, our trades-people can contribute by finding ways of improving electrical installation and plumbing techniques and our Governments can use policy to encourage energy efficient practices.

The innovative solutions to the problems we face in these areas will come from those people who have been encouraged to think creatively and who have a broad understanding of the issues – again, leading us back to that crucial initial compo-nent, our education.

Fostering creative thought and encouraging a big-picture view of the world will be the way we overcome our problems and move forward as a nation.

PETER ELLYARD

Dr Peter Ellyard is a futurist and strategist. He is Chairman of the Preferred Futures Institute and the Sustainable Prosperity Foundation, and Adjunct Professor of Intergenerational Strategies at the University of Queensland. Among his written works are *Ideas for the New Millennium* (1998, 2001) and *The Birth of Planetism* (to be published in late 2004).

BECOMING FIRST A LEADER OF SELF, THEN OF OTHERS

In my work I try to help people to get to the future first. Success will go to those who achieve it. I am reminded of comments the President of Columbia University made in the 1890s. He noted there are a few people who *make things happen*, there are rather more who *watch things happen* and there is the rest of humanity who ask *what happened*?

Much of my own work is dedicated to working with those individuals, organisations, communities and nations who find themselves in the third category and who would like to transform themselves so that they can comfortably live in the first category and thrive from doing so.

To get to the future first, one must become a leader of self. There is leadership in everybody, not just some of us. There are many so-called leaders who are making a mess of their own lives while they think they are exemplary leaders of others. The first work of leadership must be on oneself.

To get to the future first one must make three journeys. The first of these involves insight, understanding oneself.

'The secret to a successful life is to understand what it is one's destiny to do, and to do it.' (Henry Ford.)

Destiny has two elements: what one is good at, *aptitude*; and what one loves doing, *passion*. Fulfilling one's destiny defines one's *work*, doing what gives meaning to one's life. The route to success involves turning one's *work* into one's *employment*, to generate a living from doing one's work and fulfilling one's destiny.

The second journey is *foresight*: using one's imagination to travel into the future in order to access knowledge about emerging possibilities, opportunities and threats. We can understand what is unfolding through a process of what I call *Futures Questing*. Much of my work is spent on trying to understand how collections of values, or paradigms, are changing. To understand these emerging values means that I must walk into the future in my imagination.

We can predict both our industrial and economic futures, and our ethical future, by tracking how values are changing. From tracking what is happening to values we will be able to predict and understand the markets and ethics of the 21st

Century. *Future values will determine what people will find valuable and value. What people value and find valuable will determine what people will want more or less of, or want to buy and sell, what markets will form. From this we can predict what new innovations, products and services will be in demand, and made, bought or sold. This in turn will inform our ethics, what behaviours will be approved or disapproved of.*

I have developed a hypothesis about the emerging paradigm which I call *Planetism.* Planetism is the planetary version of nationalism; it involves having first allegiance to the planet.

The third journey we must take is to reflect on where we have come from, and how we arrived at where we are now. We must understand our own history and experience; *hindsight,* learning from past success and failure. I think that Australians, compared to many other cultures, have considerable difficulty in learning, becoming wise, from experience and from reflection on their experience.

'Those who do not learn from history are condemned to repeat it.' (George Santanya.)

Therefore if we wish to become a leader of ourselves and then of others in work, we undertake what I call *destiny probe (insight), futures quest (foresight)* and *wisdom search (hindsight).*

By fully embracing *insight, foresight* and *hindsight* a person can transform themselves from a life as a *future taker* and *path taker* to one of *future maker* and *path maker.*

ANTON ENUS

Anton Enus was born in apartheid South Africa in the 1960s, and has been a journalist in radio and television for over twenty years. He has filed stories from various African countries, including Congo, Zimbabwe and Rwanda. Since 1999, he's been with SBS, where he is the presenter of *World News Tonight*.

THREE STRIKES AND YOU'RE IN

KwaZulu Natal, South Africa, May 1987: The Valley of a Thousand Hills is one of the most beautiful, verdant parts of South Africa. It's the countryside brought to life in Alan Paton's epochal novel, *Cry the Beloved Country*. It's also the scene of one of the most enduring memories of my life. For it is here that thousands come each year to run the Comrade's Marathon, 90 km of undulating hills between the cities of Durban and Maritzburg.

It was somewhere beyond Drummond, I think, at about 70 km, when I hit rock bottom. Nothing had prepared me for the shock of running that distance. Body and mind were in revolt. I heard nothing, even though the people who lined the route virtually from beginning to end were shouting encouragement. At my lowest ebb I felt like the world was conspiring to make me fail. And then at my side appeared a woman of almost sixty. She wasn't your typical athletic type. In fact, she was quite round, with short legs that didn't look capable of carrying her 90 km. But not only was she coping quite efficiently (certainly a lot better than this twenty-something runner in the prime of his life), she found time to give me a little pep talk, before she slowly ran out of sight ahead of me. I often think of that moment.

It's a funny old world, isn't it? Self-declared superstars and ego-stroking indulgences abound, encouraging us to take for granted the comfort zones we create for ourselves. But every so often there's a little reminder about the true balance of things, a little strike at the heart to remind us that our best human quality is humility.

Journal entry, Malawi, May 1999: We stopped for lunch on the road to Lilongwe and were immediately besieged by what seemed like the entire local population – children and adults alike. We weren't sure whether to feel embarrassed, awkward or amused as we chomped away at our cheese sandwiches, while many eyes followed our every move. We found a loaf of stale bread that was going to be tossed out and instead gave it to these people. Well, it almost caused a riot as eager hands grabbed for a piece. I felt really uncomfortable watching children stuff huge chunks into their mouths so that others wouldn't snatch it from them. Stale, dry bread!

I spotted a young girl standing a little way from the throng. She seemed either too shy or too dignified to join the melee. I walked over to her and offered her my sandwich. She hesitated for a moment, then shyly took it. Was I doing this more for myself than for her? Myself, I guess, because it made me feel a little less awkward. Later, as we drove off, the girl looked up and I waved at her. I felt depressed about Africa.

Another strike at the heart. But does it, I wondered, lead anywhere? Was there some kind of small club in which membership is reserved for people who finally hit on the realisation that they're not such big deals after all?

Journal entry, Rishikesh India, July 1999: As I write, I see before me an old man clad in white bathing in the Ganges. He rhythmically bends forward in waist-high water and rapidly submerges his torso in the fast-flowing current. Then he ritualistically scoops up handfuls of the holy water and drinks. It's an act that to a foreigner seems ill advised. I've seen what goes into the Ganges: the cow faeces, the soap powder, the flowers, the fetid rubbish, the crowds of worshippers. Yet so many people are drawn by the supposed mythical powers of the river, which is believed to purge itself of all the detritus.

Now I see another man at the edge of the water. He is squatting and clearly exercising his bowel movements. Whatever romantic notion I'd previously held about joining the locals in a symbolic immersion in these brown waters is, I fear, rapidly diminishing.

The river, it has to be said, is a very powerful phenomenon. Just now there is a dusty, metallic quality to it as the afternoon monsoonal downpour adds to its already engorged form. The current in the middle surges by, unstoppable. Ritual bathers stick to the knee-deep edges lest they be swept away like their floating floral offerings. It's the perfect metaphor: voluntary submersion and heartfelt submission; India's lesson to the world.

Strike three. Three strikes and you're in.

CAROL FALLOWS

When Carol Fallows had her first baby in 1977 she was reading overseas parenting magazines and wondering why there was no Australian magazine. She approached a major publisher who told her no one would buy it and so, together with her partner and husband, she published the first issue of Australia's *Parents* magazine. It sold out. Over the next ten years the market grew, other magazines were published and Carol was asked to write her first book for Penguin. Since 1977 she has written fourteen books for parents and parents-to-be and had two more children. She has also written a book close to her heart, *Love & War: Stories of War Brides from the Great War to Vietnam*, as well as one-third of a health encyclopaedia.

I believe I am quite a bossy person – my mother often told me I was and I think being the eldest of three girls helped me hone my skills. I believe I am also a busybody – I like to know what's going on, where, who's involved, and why. It is these character-istics that led me into writing and editing magazines. So when it came to tackling the subject of my own beliefs I decided to use one of the devices magazine writers often find successful – I'd turn the topic into a list. So here it is – five important things I believe in – not in any order.

1. Love
Loving and being loved are the best cushions. My greatest loves are my family and friends. I have an incredibly patient, clever husband of thirty-two years without whom I would not be writing this! I have three children who, as adults, I also rate amongst my best friends – for me the greatest enjoyment comes from their company. I am currently loving observing my nineteen-year-old daughter madly in love.

2. Knowledge is power
I believe that people have a right to know the facts and to make up their own minds once they do. And I really enjoy gathering information and putting it into an easily accessible format. I also enjoy learning – in the last four years I have been learning Argentinian tango, never having done more than jiggled up and down in time to popular music in the past – and it is so rewarding. There is so much to find out and so little time – I will often lose a whole day following a trail of knowledge round the Internet.

3. Luck
I believe I am a very lucky person. I believe very much in luck and that 'there but for the grace of God go I'. At the time of the disappearance of Azaria Chamberlain, the third child of a religious couple on a camping holiday in central Australia, I was the parent of two young children. At no time could I believe that Lindy Chamberlain had murdered her

baby. For me it was always the dingo who took her baby and I felt very strongly at the time that this could have happened to any Australian family – ours included. I feel the same about the way our current government is treating refugee families who bravely take to sea in leaky boats only to be imprisoned when they reach our shores.

4. *It is worth trying to make things happen*
Five years ago we lost the business we had spent eighteen years building up – partly through bad luck, partly through mismanagement – mine included. We had to make things happen, to make a new life. It's been hard and we are not out of the mire yet, but we now live in a part of Sydney I never dreamed we could and have started a new, completely different business. Some things have worked out for us, some have not, but it has certainly been worth trying.

5. *Seizing the moment*
One of our very best friends was killed in a heli-copter accident in 1982 – we had just renewed our friendship and been on a holiday with him which made it all the more poignant, but also helped us to cope with his untimely death. Two years ago one of my dearest friends died suddenly and unexpectedly – we were very different in many ways, but we both had families we had watched grow together and we would talk for hours about many things. I miss her dreadfully, but before she died I had made the effort

to spend extra time with her, I just knew I had to. I learnt about seizing the moment from an Aboriginal lady I worked with at the ABC and I have never forgotten it.

MARTIN FLANAGAN

Martin Flanagan is a poet, author and journalist. He has published nine books. His first play opened in Melbourne in October 2004. He lives in Melbourne with his wife, two daughters and two dogs. He believes every writer should have a dog.

I know that if I look for goodness in the world I can find it. I know if I looked for badness in the world I can find that too, but I don't need to go looking for it. Each night, on the television news, I see a seemingly intractable catalogue of woes from around the globe. While I don't believe we can ignore what is going on in the world or wish away bad news, I don't think we help anyone, including ourselves, by getting depressed. As a journalist and as a writer, I take my philosophy from the 17th Century Japanese poet Basho. He wrote:

> Come, see
> real flowers
> of this painful world.

I believe real flowers exist. I've seen them and considered it my duty to record what I've seen. How many examples do I need to give you to prove my point? How many stories do you want? I've written hundreds, if not thousands, of them. Maybe my belief comes back to the fact that my father was on the Burma Railway with Weary Dunlop. That means that, as a relatively young man, my father experienced brutality, degradation, malnutrition, overwork and disease but, in Weary, he also saw an individual who overcame all of the above and inspired others to do likewise. Or maybe my philosophy comes back to the fact that the world is never as I imagine it to be. Sometimes, unforgettably, it's worse, but often – to my delight – it's better. Not in big ways, not in the ways that make headlines, but in little ways. Not long ago, my father pulled out my two stories he most liked from nearly twenty-five years of writing. One was about football, a mutual interest. The other was about a man who had grown up in an orphanage. Now he was looking after his elderly wife who had no memory, owing to Alzheimer's disease. It was one of his two favourites not because of any cleverness on my part but because of the essence of the story – a man who had little or no love growing up steadfastly refusing to abandon love.

I know that goodness may not always win. I know that often it doesn't. But it's my belief, based on hard observation, that it is never entirely defeated either. The world is not a happy or peaceful place but for all its unease there is a miracle at work in its doings and that miracle, that hope, is the cause I choose to serve.

NIKKI GEMMELL

Nikki Gemmell is the author of *Shiver*, *Cleave*, *Love Song* and *The Bride Stripped Bare*; and her short stories appear in numerous literary journals. She was born in Wollongong and now lives in London.

This I believe.

That a life driven by love is preferable to a life driven by greed or ambition.

That desire is a much more robust concept than I've sometimes given it credit for.

That with sex, honesty is the most shocking thing of all.

That it's amazing how much support you get when you tell the truth.

That it's wise to distance yourself from people who want to flatten you. I've been hurt again and again over the years by several friends – and it's only now I've found the strength to say no, enough. I want to be surrounded by heart-lifters, not heart-sinkers.

That kindness is life-affirming. It can crack my heart. It's about lowering ourselves, as is being interested in someone – giving them the gift of attention, asking them questions. 'Vivacity is surrender,' said Les Murray, and why should that seem so demeaning?

That the most intense happiness is to be found in the simplest things: the sight of your father laughing uncontrollably during a film, a bedroom filled with the sleep of your children, requited love.

That Alice Springs is my Great Good Place. (A GGP is a Henry James term, denoting a cherished place that brings you to stillness and calm.)

That a woman is sexy if she thinks she is.

That having children puts you at the coalface of living, and as a writer, that's a good place to be. Motherhood didn't turn out to be the professional impediment I expected; children have dragged me into life.

That a lot of women are still subservient to their partner's pleasure at the expense of their own. Why? Because we don't want them to turn away from us, perhaps; we don't want them to find the women who love giving blow jobs; we want them to think we're someone else. And because sometimes we're willing to put up with a lot, to preserve a relationship – and to have children. For many women that's a deeply biological urge that no amount of feminist empowerment is going to circumvent.

That my father's mother will never forgive me for asking my mother to walk me down the aisle.

That after several years of marriage and two children in quick succession my husband stopped looking at me. I was confronted with a new sense of erasure. What to do? I wrote an explicit book about sex within marriage. There was a result I hadn't anticipated: my husband started noticing me again.

That writing hurts.

That I gravitate towards people who've suffered in some way – it's as if their edges have been softened by some sort of sorrow.

That rupture is good.

That shared sleep is deeply sexy, often more so than making love. It's where true love lies, beyond words, beyond sex. I can imagine a time when I may lose my taste for sex, but I'll never lose my desire for shared sleep.

That it's healthier in a relationship to be wanted rather than needed.

That it's extremely hard to seduce someone who's content. You need dissatisfaction, uncertainty, insecurity for an affair.

That there's not a person alive who doesn't want to be told they're loved.

That a great solace, and stillness, can be found in faith. It helps me to let go.

That to be truly free you have to stop worrying about what other people think of you.

That at the end of our lives the question should be not what we have done, but how well we have loved.

TRISTAN GIBLIN

Tristan Giblin is a seventeen-year-old who lives in Hobart, Tasmania but would like to live somewhere where something actually happens. His interests lie in soccer, which he is not at all good at but loves to play, and reading, through which he gained a love for writing. He also enjoys watching TV. He is a teenager after all. He prefers to write action/adventure stories but doesn't mind the occasional essay. Only if it's not a school essay of course. After school he hopes to either keep writing or to direct films, which are another thing he loves to watch.

> In the beginning was the Word . . . and the Word was God.
>
> > New Testament, John 1.1.

There has always been a debate in my mind about whether or not I believe in God. This debate has intensified after I was invited to contribute to *I Believe This*. I find it very probable that there was a man who called himself Jesus Christ, but was he the Son of God? Does God really exist? We all know of the impossible feats that Jesus supposedly accomplishes in The Bible. I believe that these legends started out as minor things that he was seen doing and through time have been greatly exaggerated. The thing I find ironic though is Jesus lived in the Middle-Eastern area, which is the area that today has very many varied religions. Judaism, Islam and Buddhism to name but a few. So yes, I do believe in Jesus, but do I believe in God? This is where it gets complicated.

I believe in God as a spiritual state of mind rather than a being. This state of mind is very difficult to attain and requires complete devotion; I believe it cannot be attained whilst living. I believe it is almost like a good dream that starts for the devoted when their life ends. The freeing of the mind from the body and being free is one of the things that I believe most strongly in. Spiritual freedom is a crucial part of being human.

Physical freedom is a right that we all deserve, especially refugees and political prisoners who are being detained against their will. If these people have just escaped from war or religious persecution the first thing the government should do is try to console them. Locking them up only adds to the trauma. I am very lucky to have been blessed and born into a relatively well-off family in an excellent country such as Australia. I value my freedom very much after watching a documentary on TV about life inside a maximum-security prison. It followed the story of a man who was sexually molested every day and to escape it he had to mutilate himself to be allowed entry to the infirmary. This taught me to value my freedom above all else.

Perhaps not above everything though, I also believe strongly in my family. My family is very important to me; my parents brought me into this world, for which I am eternally grateful. They raised me and taught me all the important lessons life holds. If I had just one day to live, the first and most important thing for me would be to make peace with my family and convey to them my love. Making peace usually requires just a simple word – but some people find it impossible to say the word 'sorry'.

Words themselves are very important to me. I gained a passion for writing through reading, which I believe is one of the best forms of entertainment ever. Stories involve imagination and mental images. Stories also link generations. To write stories we need words. We learn them at a very young age and we use them every day. They are what make us the most intelligent beings on the planet. They differentiate us from other life forms. Words are what make us human.

I do not believe there is a simple 'meaning of life.' I do not believe that God created man; we just evolved from the apes. All life is a cycle of events on the way to death. We are born, we live, we die. I do not believe in the afterlife, so this means that we have to make life good. It is a gift; we have to try to enjoy it, because after this there is nothing more. I believe death is final. Like a computer shutting down, it just switches us off, no memory left. Nothing left. Life is like the moving walkways they have at the airports, just a lot longer. No matter what happens, you have to move on. The quicker you get over the hardships in your life, the quicker you can get on with it.

In the beginning was the word. Who knows what's at the end?

PETER GOLDSWORTHY

Peter Goldsworthy grew up in various country towns, finishing his schooling in Darwin. He lives in Adelaide, where he spends his mornings writing and his afternoons working as a general practitioner. He is the chair of the Libraries Board of South Australia, and of the Literature Board of the Australia Council. His most recent novel is *Three Dog Night*. His *Collected Stories* was published by Penguin in May 2004.

I believe I will never find an answer to two fundamental mysteries.

One: why is there something rather than nothing?

Two: what is consciousness, and how could it arise in a world of unconscious matter?

These are the boundaries that surround our more concrete and everyday world – the final frontiers of human curiosity. Like the edges of our visual fields that vanish into a mysterious nothingness they are both eerie and difficult to notice. A little less mysterious, but more urgently pressing, is the question of how to live in the everyday world inside those weird boundaries.

People say we live in a Judeo-Christian culture. I can't see that. Our culture is built on science, and scepticism. It owes more to Socrates than to Moses or Christ. I believe in scepticism – the institution-alised scepticism of science. It causes tremendous problems, but only it can solve them. Perhaps I spent too much of my childhood in too many Sunday schools, but I loathe all piety – although holier-than-thou piety these days seems to come less from the religious than the morally and politically pious.

I believe in humour – for its hedge against those mysterious darknesses outside our ken, and for its mental health.

I'm not sure why I believe we must treat others as we would be treated ourselves. Evolutionary game-playing models have shown that this is a useful and optimal survival strategy. Its altruisms apparently evolved in our brains for good reasons. I can see why love evolved in our brains, likewise – but it still feels marvellous.

From Socrates, I take my belief in the examined, sceptical life. As unhappy as it sometimes makes me, the pleasures of its illuminations far outweigh its disillusionments.

And there is no other intellectually honest path.

POSIE GRAEME-EVANS

Named by *Variety* magazine as one of 'twenty significant international women in film and television' in December 2002, Posie Graeme-Evans has been a producer, director and writer for over twenty-five years and in 2001 was chosen as the inaugural 'Australian Independent Producer of the Year'. Creator, song-lyricist and initiating producer of *McLeod's Daughters* – winner of four Logie awards in 2004, including 'Most Popular Drama' and 'Most Popular Australian Program' – and co-creator of *Hi-5*, with Helena Harris, Posie published her first novel *The Innocent* in November 2002, followed by *The Exiled* in November 2003. Both books have become bestsellers. Posie is now writing the untitled third part in this trilogy set in 15th Century England and progressive world-wide publication has begun with *The Innocent*, in April 2004, in the US. Posie is married to her business and creative partner Andrew Blaxland, lives in Sydney and is currently Director of Drama for the Nine network and a very proud granny of Rohan (three) and Toby (one) Mackellar.

I make drama and write books because I am end-lessly interested in why we do the things we do. And who we are. *What* we are.

I think (at the moment) that the essence of being human has not changed from even the most ancient times. We just eat different food and wear different clothes. And believe equally strange things.

We still want what our ancestors wanted and are driven by the same desires and confusions; and you and I know all about them: love versus lust, God versus mammon, self-interest versus self sacrifice, duty versus what you really want, courage versus cowardice – and so on. And for each excellent, life-affirming quality there's the tricky attraction of the dark side. That duel is the script of my life.

Personally, I think you feel better about yourself, in the long run, if you can side with the angels more often than walk in the dark. But, what would I know? Don't judge other people's lives; that's a big one and very, very hard to achieve.

What else?

Well, I think effective contraception is the single greatest change that human society might ever see: half the human race is choosing its own destiny by not having a baby a year.

Yet I believe in having kids: I've had one, been given others, and I discover that I love them more and more yearningly as time goes on (and God knows, he she it or them, that I fell in love with my daughter at her birth). And each time my grandson says 'I love you, Nonnie' I'm a puddle on the floor.

In the end, however, I think sex, and what people will do to get it, could be the most powerful force at work in our world (yes, there's religion, and hunger and terrorism, and, and . . . but still . . .).

Yet I *know*, and you know too, that sex, in the end, ain't no substitute for love – that complex, complex little word which has more strength than water and earthquakes. If you're lucky (and I do believe in luck) I think that the peace and meaning a long-term relationship brings is possible. It had better be or we're all stuffed!

Sift everything down and I believe that life is risk – each day, each moment, the veneer between the peaceful present and chaos is very thin. But I think that's good; it's stimulating, and terror's always made me concentrate quite productively, given my short attention span. Bring on the earthquake! (Just kidding.)

But I, like many others, also wrestle with what it means to live a good life. It feels so hard to get things right, even for a moment, because my temperament yearns for black and white, wants simplicity and clarity, and a comprehensible shape to things. Ah, simplicity. Give it to me, Lord, but not yet.

However, my mother really does say 'You're never given more than you can carry' and life has demonstrated that to me. I've come to believe in the genetic bit of grit I've been handed; when things get rough, I want to run away but I find that hard to do. A blessing and a curse, a weakness and a strength, that, but it does make things happen. So, in the end, I do thank my ancestors for that bloody, mindless persistence I'm able to demonstrate – and I wonder who carried it first.

Yes, I'm grateful to them but I'd have liked to've been born blonde as well. And taller.

Believe me.

CORINNE GRANT

Corinne Grant has been working as a comedian, actor and writer since the early nineties. She is currently a cast member on television shows *Rove Live* and *The Glasshouse*. Corinne grew up in the country town of Corryong, NE Victoria, and moved to Melbourne in 1991 to attend La Trobe University. She has worked variously as a check-out chick, a secretary, an usher and as an entertainer for a nursing home in Moonee Ponds, where her specialities included playing the pianola and calling bingo.

One of my earliest memories is of talking to my grandad. I talked to him every night just before I went to sleep. I would have been about six years old, I suppose, and I used to tell him everything I had done that day. I would tell him about the egg and lettuce sandwiches my mum had made for lunch. I would tell him about the boy I sat next to who wet himself during arts and crafts and how the cleaner came in and sprinkled the wee with sawdust (I thought this was the most amazing thing I had ever seen). I would tell him about the day *I* wet myself and how I had to go to lost and found for a spare pair of knickers and all they had was a pair of 'sugarbags'. (These were giant, baggy, scratchy undies. Even at six years old, I knew they were gross.) I would tell him about the time I got the ruler across my bum for playing kiss chasey. If I had a nightmare, I would tell him all about it the next night. If something had scared me or upset me during the day, I would tell him. I told him all the things I was excited about, that I dreamed about, things I hoped would happen and things I wished wouldn't happen.

I told him about how I wanted to marry a boy from kindergarten but he now attended the Catholic School at the other end of town. Obviously, due to distance, the marriage was now off. This was a great disappointment to me as I had envisaged we would go to the same school and we would walk there together and he would carry my books just like on *Little House On The Prairie*. I hadn't thought the marriage through any further than that.

My Pa was my confidant and my friend. I wanted him to know every single detail about my life. This was very important to me. I wanted him to know everything that was going on in my world. He had died two years before I was born and there was no other way for him to know.

I knew how much my Mum had loved Pa and I felt sorry that he wasn't here with her anymore. If I told him everything, he wouldn't feel like he was missing out. Even though I had never met him, I loved him very much. My mum had filled me with this love. He was there from the start. I couldn't see him but I could feel him smiling down on me from the ceiling above my bed. Just smiling and listening.

A few years ago, I told my mum about this. Her eyes glimmered and she told me that when I was born, she felt that he was beside her. To both of us, he was still a part of the family.

This I believe: that you can love someone even if they're not here any more. That you can love someone even if you've never met them. It is this love, passed down through generations, that keeps people alive forever. I still sometimes talk to my Pa and now I talk to my Nanna as well. It means they are always with me. And I am sure they are listening.

BRADLEY TREVOR GREIVE

Born in Tasmania in 1970, Bradley Trevor Greive (BTG) went on to graduate from the Royal Military College and later served as a paratroop platoon commander before leaving the army to become one of Australia's most successful creative talents. To date BTG has written eight books with worldwide sales now in excess of 10 million copies. His books include *Priceless, The Vanishing Beauty of a Fragile Planet* and *The Blue Day Book*, which was awarded the 2000 ABA Book Of The Year.

A committed conservationist, Bradley supports wildlife projects on every continent and is also Governor of the Taronga Foundation. BTG is a passionate champion for the arts, being a proud sponsor of the Australian Youth Orchestra and also the founder and Chairman of the Taronga Foundation Poetry Prize, Australia's leading prize for young poets.

When I was a soldier I believed in many things. I believe in less now, however I believe more deeply than I did before.

Contrary to what you may have heard or suspected from reading my books, I am not necessarily an optimist by nature. I believe in people; that is true. I have witnessed more than enough kind and selfless acts in my time to feel comfortable stating that people are, by and large, good.

However there is definitely a great sadness in the world, so much so that I sometimes feel it is possible to be born with a broken heart and live a whole life of loss and sorrow without ever knowing why. That is of course assuming that you do not want to know why. At some stage we all slide complacently into the lukewarm bath of fatigue and despair, hoping that the bitter end will at least be no worse than this. And you see, this is where I become an optimist. It is a conscious choice. I choose to be an optimist because I simply see no reason to go on unless the best is yet to come.

It is not a question of blind faith, empowering though that is for many people. It is a simple case of cause and effect. The creative energy inherent in one individual is enough to change the course of history. It is certainly enough to transform the reality for that individual as well. I have seen this happen, for better or for worse, many times.

Therefore I choose to embrace the unknown.

I choose to seek light and laughter in the midst of doom and gloom.

I choose to put my shoulder to the mountain, lest it crumble at my feet.

And strangely enough I do not grow tired from this exertion. I grow stronger. My belief in myself and in others grows and grows until I feel confident that all good things are possible in good time. I observe the definitive results that true passion brings and I become more determined to direct my energies towards helping build a future that gleams brightly upon the faces of those who would greet it with me.

So many aspects of our time are in need of urgent attention. So much that has been injured or lost must be restored. Chief among these are the preservation and celebration of both our cultural and natural heritage. For too long we have not appreciated our planet's precious biodiversity and the unique voices from home and abroad. Language and life fail without love and attention. A tree without roots cannot stand. The most beautiful ballad falls without ears to hear.

We live in an age where we drown in information but desperately thirst for knowledge and wisdom. Creative thinking cannot be locked in a luminous vault with artists, writers and musicians. Everyone should be encouraged to reinvent their inner wheels. We must all champion emerging talent, however modest, in friends, family and colleagues, however old. We must shield those sparks and glowing embers, fanning the flames so that they burn brightly because of us and not in spite of us. Bringing life into this world by way of birth, art, conversation and invention is what moves us forward to a better time.

I do not long for free and easy living. There is no utopia on my horizon towards which I would set my sail. Perfection is only interesting as an ideal. I am for internal abrasion, not because this produces pearls, though it does and these are lovely, but because it stimulates introspection, growth and most importantly provokes change.

Change is the basis of life on earth. Since this planet first claimed a name the ground has literally shifted beneath our feet. Great geographic flux that, in a vast yet subtle way, perpetually mocks any attachment to political boundaries.

I believe in positive change.

I look in the mirror and see where it begins.

KATE GRENVILLE

Kate Grenville has written six books of fiction, among them the award-winning novels *Lilian's Story* and *The Idea of Perfection*. She has also written three books about the writing process, one in collaboration with Sue Woolfe. She is currently completing a novel set on the Hawkesbury River near Sydney in 1815.

Is it too shallow to say I believe in chance? A person with a formal religious belief would say there's no such thing: everything is part of God's Grand Plan. In that case 'chance' is a convenient word for meaning that we don't understand.

When I was in my twenties I went to India with a documentary film crew. It was a life-changing experience and one moment stands out as forming a part of what I believe. We were filming in a remote desert part of Rajasthan. We'd driven for several hours along dirt tracks, through a landscape of dust and sand, to a tiny village made of more dust and sand. The water supply was a hole in the ground with a concrete apron around it, where women lowered brass pots on a rope. The houses in the village were huts no bigger than kids' cubbies. In the school a dozen children in dust-coloured clothes sat on the concrete floor, the sum total of each child's equipment a little piece of slate to write on. The fields all around seemed to contain only dust and sand with the occasional goat nibbling at a thorny bush. It was poverty of a kind I could hardly understand, and lives so narrow and without prospects that they were unimaginable.

All the women we'd seen wore the tail of their sari up over their heads to cover their faces, but as we walked along a path between two fields of dust, a woman of about my own age came towards us and, as she passed me, she let the veil blow back from her face for a moment and we looked into each others' eyes. In that moment, before she pulled the veil back, I thought, This woman is myself. What I meant was, in that exchange of glances there was an instinctive recognition of a fellow-soul. She could have been in my shoes, I could have been in hers. Chance had landed her here, in this dry hopeless place, as it had landed me in plush Australia, but in that piercing moment I could see that was all it was – chance.

I think now that her life probably had its joys and satisfactions – in my ignorance I couldn't guess at them. But the insight of that moment has remained with me – that no matter how 'other' the other seems, we're all part of the same web of human life.

Some of us get to live a soft life and others spend their lives in the hard stony places of the world. Poverty is by no means the worst thing that happens in many of those hard places. People try to kill you and your family and you have to run for your life to some place of safety – Australia, maybe.

I believe that we who live the good life need to remember the humbling truth that we did nothing to earn it and nothing to deserve it. In a world of chance we have a moral duty to try to treat those 'others' as we'd hope to be treated ourselves – with humanity and understanding. We're part of each other in this world, and a wrong done to another demeans and damages all of us.

ANDY GRIFFITHS

Andy Griffiths is an Australian author. His books include *The Day My Bum Went Psycho* and *Zombie Bums from Uranus* as well as the extremely popular 'JUST' series of short stories which were adapted as a twenty-six episode television cartoon series called *What's With Andy?* Andy's books have won numerous children's choice awards. His books *Just Disgusting!* and *Zombie Bums from Uranus* topped both the children's and adult bestseller lists when they were released in Australia, and *The Day My Butt Went Psycho* and *Zombie Butts from Uranus* are both *New York Times* bestsellers.

> to be nobody but yourself – in a world which is doing its best, night and day, to make you like everybody else – means to fight the hardest battle which any human being can fight, and never stop fighting
>
> e.e.cummings

While human beings have much in common, every person has a unique combination of skills, perspective and experience that makes them utterly unlike anybody else who ever lived. I believe that the most important thing a person can do for their own well-being, as well as the greater well-being of society, is to discover exactly what their unique qualities are and to give them the fullest possible expression. For a few fortunate people the path is clear from an early age. For others – perhaps the majority – it is a little less obvious.

My own search didn't begin in earnest until the age of twenty-eight, when I left a secure, very enjoyable job as an English teacher in a Victorian country high school and returned to Melbourne to try to make a living as a writer. I didn't know how I was going to do it, what I was going to write or whether it would even be possible to make a living from writing (many people assured me that it wouldn't), but I knew I would get no peace from the little voice inside me until I'd at least given it a try.

Over three years as a teacher I'd managed to save enough money to support myself for at least one year, maybe two at a pinch . . . about the time I estimated it would take to discover 'the secret to getting published', which I was certain all published writers possessed. In pursuit of this secret I read every book on the craft of writing I could find. I went to hear as many writers speak as possible. I enrolled in every writing class that was going. But as I searched I began to notice a strange thing. Every writer appeared to be saying something slightly different. Every writer seemed to have their own particular way of doing things. It began to dawn on me that maybe, just maybe, there was no 'secret'. Or if there was a secret, it was this: every writer invents their own way.

I started to loosen up. Instead of writing in the way I imagined that 'published writers' wrote, I began to let my sense of humour come through. Instead of writing about the subjects and ideas that I imagined 'published writers' wrote about, I began to write about the subjects and ideas that interested, concerned and/or amused me. At first it felt a little perverse and even foolhardy – a fact which many publishers were only too happy to confirm in the many rejection letters I received (e.g. 'Interesting material, but we can't see an existing market for this'). I was concerned, but not unduly. I figured that the fact that they couldn't see an 'existing' market for what I was writing might just possibly mean that I was on the right track. And, besides, exploring this idiosyncratic territory had become such an absorbing and enjoyable process in itself, that even if the writing were never published I thought at least I'd die happy, having spent my time doing what was mine to do, exploring what was mine to explore and expressing what was mine to express. As it turned out it was the best decision I could have made. It did, however, take more like ten hard years to get to the position where I could make a living from writing rather than the one or two I originally imagined: but hey, better ten than never.

I see many people wander through their lives never realising the unique gifts that are theirs and theirs alone to bring to the world. They shy away from anything that might cause them to challenge their comfortable assumptions about themselves, content to allow a combination of fear, circumstances, and other people's opinions and expectations of them to shape their ideas about what's possible. I believe it's never too early – or late – to start asking the questions: 'What is it that really absorbs me?' and 'What am I uniquely suited to being able to contribute to both my life and the lives of others?' – and then to have the courage, patience and persistence to act on the answers as if your life depends on it. Because, in a very real sense, it does.

Ian Hamilton-Craig

Dr Hamilton-Craig is the Chairman of MEDPED-FH (Australia) and recently established the Genetic Cholesterol Foundation of Australia. He is a Fellow of the Royal Australasian College of Physicians, the Cardiac Society of Australia and New Zealand, and the Linnean Society of London. He has written several medical books for the general public: *Cholesterol Control* (1987), *Men's Health* (1992), *Bypass* (1997) and *State of the Heart – Controlling Cholesterol and Triglycerides* (2004). In 1999 he was jointly awarded the RT Hall Prize for the most significant contribution to Australian cardiovascular research.

In my early youth I was intrigued by, and indeed felt a vague sense of disquiet in, my mother's fatalistic attitude to life.

She believed that everything was part of a wonderful, but unalterable, Grand Plan. Her philosophy was simply 'do unto others as you would have them do unto you'.

Having been brought up on one hand with such traditional Christian philosophy, and on the other by a highly scientific education, I am the true Piscean, swimming in two directions, a mixture of family upbringing and the acquired scientific knowledge of the objective worlds of chemistry, mathematics, physics and biology.

This – perhaps – has provided me with an open mind on some of the larger issues of life, and a degree of healthy scepticism for traditional dogma.

My career in medical practice has taught me that life is a fragile thing, like a leaf trembling on a bough blown by strong winds, threatening to break off in an instant.

At the same time, I am aware that basic laws of science (including probability) govern our bodies. We are beginning to understand the biochemical mechanisms of health and disease, including the genetic metabolic disorders. This understanding can help to alter our own health destinies and outwit – for a time at least – the genes which otherwise would determine our fate.

My own special area is the role of cholesterol in heart disease, and I have a particular interest in the genetic cholesterol disorders. One of these is the genetic familial hypercholesterolaemia (FH), which is characterised by very high cholesterol levels. If untreated, people with FH can suffer from heart attack and even early death in their forties or fifties. Sometimes, tragically, the first sign of disease is sudden death.

My friend, the late Professor Roger Williams of Utah, US, likened FH to being a passenger on a plane destined to crash, for which one received one's ticket at birth as part of a genetic package. 'Every year in the US', he would say, 'one jumbo jet full of FH people crashes, and all its passengers are killed'.

He believed, however, that early death from FH

was preventable, and FH people did not have to board that tragic flight. He therefore espoused community-wide screening of cholesterol levels in children, so that FH could be diagnosed early and treated effectively. He set up the MEDPED (Make Early Diagnosis, Prevent Early Deaths) program, which now has branches in over thirty-four countries around the world.

I never felt quite comfortable with Roger's aeroplane metaphor, and when Roger died in a plane crash on the way to a MEDPED meeting in Europe, it seemed to me one of the very saddest ironies of fate.

I believe, however, that the 'genetic marked card' of FH can now be altered, and the outcome changed. We are able to combat the gene for FH, and can overcome the fatalistic attitudes of the days before family cholesterol screening. People with FH used to say to me, 'All my uncles died in their forties, so I will too'. They awaited the inevitable advance of disease. Now advances in science, translated into everyday medical practice, make such fatalism outdated. Their disease can be halted. They can reach a normal lifespan.

I am enormously encouraged that people are living to see their own grandchildren in families where this has never before happened . It strengthens my belief in the positive role of preventative medicine, in passion for humanitarian causes, and in ongoing scientific research for the benefit of mankind.

NICHOLAS HASLUCK

Nicholas Hasluck has published ten works of fiction including the prize-winning novels *The Bellarmine Jug* and *The Country Without Music.* He served as Chair of the Literature Board of the Australia Council from 1998 to 2001 and is presently a Judge of the Supreme Court of Western Australia.

The most intriguing book to come out of the Great War was *Her Privates We*, a novel recording the author's experience on the Somme front in 1916. The book, by Private 19022, contains a harrowing account of men living in a state of constant apprehension, disoriented by the hubbub of battle, adrift in a chaotic world. No one seems to know the battle plan; orders from above don't square with the realities below; trenches lead nowhere; normal codes of conduct are meaningless.

Affected by all of this, struggling to find a way through the confusion, the narrator is momentarily arrested by a random thought: 'If a man could not be certain of himself, he could be certain of nothing.'

The author of the book, his identity masked by a peculiar nom-de-plume, had obviously fought alongside ordinary foot soldiers and endured the privations of battle at the lowest level. And yet, the title points to an arcane literary allusion. It echoes a bawdy exchange between Hamlet and Guildenstern. When Hamlet acknowledges that 'on fortune's cap we are not the very button', and hence we must 'live about her waist, or in the middle of her favours', the bewildered Guildenstern responds: 'Faith, her privates we.' Perhaps the author of *Her Privates We* meant by this that in the end men and women are governed essentially not by reason or by high ideals, but by their instincts. They are transient flesh and blood.

The anonymous author turned out to be the Australian expatriate, Frederic Manning, a quiet, reclusive intellectual who had mixed with Ezra Pound and others in pre-war London literary circles. He never became well-known as a writer but his novel is still regarded as a masterpiece.

The extremities described in Manning's book lie far beyond my own experience, but it doesn't take much experience to understand that the simple codes of conduct propounded in the classroom or at Sunday school are insufficient for the complexities of life as an adult. Young and impressionable, adrift in a chaotic world, pushed and pulled by private whims, the expectations of others, and a host of competing forces, I quickly concluded that I would have to rely on my own judgment about the right thing to do in each case, becoming conscious as the years went by that the way to go was usually deter- mined by instinct. Principles that suit one person can be disastrous for another. Most opinions (including one's own) turn out to be simply an echo of the prevailing mood.

If a man could not be certain of himself, he could be certain of nothing.

Manning favours the sceptical outlook, the refusal to take anything for granted, the need to look at things in the light of one's own experience. As another character in *Hamlet* puts it: 'To thine ownself be true, and thou canst not then be false to any man.'

Do precepts of this kind lead to vanity and self-interest? I think not. A person is more likely to become vainglorious – the very button on fortune's cap – when he or she has surrendered to fashion, and begins to measure achievement by the adulation of the group. To my mind, the less conspicuous 'private', who has become aware of his or her limitations by a gradual process of self-knowledge, is better placed than the other to become a fully rounded person and contribute to the wisdom of the group, for the random flow of private observations will inevitably be linked to entanglements in the surrounding world, until, in the end, the observer feels obliged to remove the reclusive mask and speak out. As Frederic Manning did – with lasting effect.

STEVEN HEATHCOTE

Steven Heathcote, AM, first studied ballet with Shelly Rae and Kira Bousloff in his home-town of Perth. He then graduated from The Australian Ballet School in 1982 and joined The Australian Ballet in 1983; he was promoted to Soloist in 1985, Senior Artist in 1986 and to the rank of Principal in 1987. Steven Heathcote has an extensive repertoire of principal roles and has created leading roles in many world premiere ballets.

In addition to his overseas tours with The Australian Ballet, he has made guest appearances with companies such as American Ballet Theatre, Birmingham Royal Ballet, Ballet Nacional de Cuba, the Kirov Ballet and the Royal Danish Ballet. He has partnered international ballerinas Susan Jaffe, Nina Ananiashvili and Alessandra Ferri.

In 1991 Steven was appointed a Member of the Order of Australia for his services to dance and in 1995 received the Mo Award for Dance Performer of the Year. In 2001 he received the inaugural Helpmann Award for Best Male Dancer, and again in 2002 for his portrayal of Albrecht in *Giselle*. He has just completed his 20th year with The Australian Ballet, for which anniversary Stephen Page created the solo work *Totem*.

In 2003, Steven was awarded Best Male Dancer at the Green Room Awards, and again received the Mo Award for Dance Performer of the Year, for his role in Graeme Murphy's critically acclaimed *Swan Lake*.

I believe that the person I am today exists because of the influence of many people.

All along the way, I have come into contact with people who **believed in me**.

At the age of nine I came home from watching my first ballet performance at the Perth Concert Hall and announced to my Mum that I wanted to be a dancer . . . She **believed** me and some months later sourced the most highly regarded teacher she could find, Madame Kira Bousloff, who had a great passion for dance. Madame said to me more than once that she **believed** I would do great things with my dancing.

When my commitment to dance classes began to waver during teenage years, my parents gently encouraged me to persist, because they **believed** that I could transcend the doubt and come out the other side stronger and more committed because I had learned the value of perseverance.

At around thirteen or fourteen years old, my second teacher Shelley Rae Aris told me that she **believed** I would be one of Australian Ballet's top Principal Dancers one day.

After auditioning for the Australian Ballet School at the age of fifteen, Dame Margaret Scott, then director of the school, said she **believed** I had all the right material for the school and offered me a place for the following year.

So now my parents were faced with the prospect of letting their fifteen-year-old son travel from Perth to Melbourne to start an entirely new life with only a couple of months to prepare. Once again they **believed** I could do it and did everything they could to support me as I embarked upon the biggest journey I had ever undertaken.

In 1983 I commenced dance studies at the Australian Ballet School and found myself surrounded by many dancers of an exceptionally high standard. This was the best thing that could have happened, because suddenly, the benchmark was raised considerably.

I realised then, the most important thing was to exercise my own belief in myself and my capacity to rise to the many challenges that would occur over the ensuing years.

It would have been considerably harder to find that **self belief** were it not for the confidence my parents and teachers had in me through earlier developmental years.

I was also very fortunate to have teachers at the Ballet School who were inspirational and once again, expressed a **belief** in my abilities.

After two years at the School, Marilyn Rowe, the Australian Ballet Company director, saw something in me that she **believed** would develop. She had enough confidence in me to offer me a contract, something I had dreamed about and aspired to for many years.

Her successor, Maina Gielgud, was to have the

most significant impact on the development of my career, and her **belief** in me spelled the beginning of the most accelerated and successful period of my dancing life.

What all this means to me now after twenty-one fulfilling years with the Australian Ballet is that when I am coaching young dancers or just talking with them, it's important that I let them know I have confidence and **belief** in their abilities. As a parent this is something I see as crucial to the future of my children; most importantly, encouraging them to find that little voice within that says, Yes, I can do this. It might be challenging, frustrating or even frightening, but if I just get in there, put my head down, tail up and believe in myself, then I can do anything!

So, if you ask me what I believe, it is in the power of belief itself.

Elizabeth Hepburn

Liz Hepburn IBVM is a member of the Institute of the Blessed Virgin Mary (Loreto Sisters). She lives in Canberra and works there for Catholic Health Australia as the Director of Ministry and Ethics. She is in her mid-fifties, has encountered her mortality but keeps fit through walking, swimming and drinking moderate amounts of red wine with friends.

Once I was at a workshop in which we were asked to identify qualities which we would say were uniquely ours, and to write these on the leaves of a branch we had been instructed to bring with us. After a quiet period in which we all undertook this seriously, we were asked to talk to one other person about how we felt. It was extremely confronting.

The final stage of the exercise was to go outside and to strip our branch of its leaves, saying as we discarded the leaves, 'I am Liz Hepburn, an honest woman, and I am no longer "honest"'. It was to bring us to the realisation that we have a tenuous hold on life, and that even though we prize aspects of ourselves as possessions, that is something of an illusion: all is a gift. It was powerful for everyone involved.

Although the workshop ran from 9 am until 6 pm every day for a week, and 150 adults did the most extraordinary things together, that was the exercise which brought me to a profound realisation of my creatureliness. It is a lesson which I have needed to have repeated, I am ashamed to say. For there is in me an inordinate desire to exercise mastery over myself. This workshop led me to admit the error of this outlook.

Every gift has a giver and a recipient. As recipient I needed to acknowledge the gift and the giver. Then to ask for what purpose the gift was given because I could not believe it was given without purpose. The purpose is to try to live as transparently as possible, to make my search for meaning available for all to see. This is difficult for an introvert.

When Loreto sisters make perpetual vows, it is customary to take a verse from the Bible as a motto. I took as my motto the words 'Only connect', from E.M. Forster. The entire section reads:

Only connect the prose and the passion, and both will be exalted, and human love will be seen at its height. Live in fragments no longer.

As a scientist, I longed to forge links between the prose and passion of my life; to live in fragments no longer. 'Only connect' seemed to give direction and unity to this insane quest on which I was embarking.

Having made the connection between the gift and the giver, it seemed obvious, in a way, that gifts were for others. In a way, the gifts only made sense in a relational setting, for they would be neither recognised nor given a chance to be seen, except in community. In a real sense we need each other.

My own community of family and friends has sustained me thus far on the journey. Along with them I have sought to understand the world and what is required of us to build it up. I have learned to treasure the moments, the seemingly small, inconsequential gains we have made. Not to despair that we appear to have made little progress in arranging a more just distribution of the world's heritage.

I believe that we all have gifts to be directed towards the building of the world, in which opposing forces will become aligned in harmony. That these gifts will only be called forth and expressed by a community which knows itself in need of all gifts. That in a paradoxical sense by developing these gifts in and for the community we will finally become the people we can be, and we will experience great peace in this. That the alignment of human longings and desires and the well being of the universe at large can and will occur when we all accept that we are beloved.

SCOTT HICKS

Scott Hicks is an internationally acclaimed film-maker and screen writer and has been nominated for and won many prestigious awards for his work. His 1996 film *Shine* was an international box office sensation and was nominated for seven Academy Awards, including Best Director and Best Original Screenplay, with Geoffrey Rush winning Best Actor. *Shine* also received BAFTA and AFI awards and nominations from the Golden Globes, the Directors Guild of America and the Writers Guild of America. Hicks' *Snow Falling on Cedars* (1999) was also nominated for an Academy Award. He received an Emmy for his documentary series *Submarines: Sharks of Steel* in 1994, and his film *Sebastian and the Sparrow* (1988) won at three international film festivals for children. His most recent film was *Hearts in Atlantis* (2001), starring Anthony Hopkins. Scott graduated from Flinders University in South Australia in 1975 and was awarded an honorary doctorate in 1997. Born and raised in East Africa, Scott and his wife Kerry Heysen live in Adelaide, as do their two sons.

I became a filmmaker quite by accident. Not for me a childhood squinting through the family camera – my early dramas were of a different order! In Kenya, where I grew up, there was no television in the sixties, and aside from the occasional drive-in excursion, trips to the cinema were rare. Not that we lacked enter-tainment – family 'safaris', school cricket matches interrupted by herds of antelope, the cycle of flood, drought and famine that was the drama of African life.

At boarding school, we were treated to Friday night screenings of worthy subjects like Olivier's *Hamlet*, with occasionally racier stories like *Maneaters of Tsavo* to leaven the fare. So by the time I turned up to study Drama at Flinders University in South Australia, I was essentially an 'image deprived' youth of sixteen.

As a consequence, I suddenly developed a kind of gluttony for imagery and cinematic ideas. It was no longer enough to troop out with the family to the annual *Lawrence of Arabia* or Bond spectacular. To my parents' benign bewilderment I was off to flea-pit cinemas nightly to catch the latest 'ini' film – Fellini, Pasolini, Antonioni, Bergman. And the minor topic of filmmaking in my drama course proved the Demon Seed – bursting open to colonise my entire Honours degree. Filmmaking was simply the most fun thing to do with my friends – I had no idea you could make a living from it, indeed that didn't seem to be the point.

What did seem important was listening to that inner voice that was guiding me, such as in the very choice of my university course. I had actually applied to enrol in a Law/Arts degree at Adelaide University, when I saw a rock musical about the Vietnam war. At the show's end, a forum was announced to discuss the issues – to be chaired by some academic from a place called Flinders University. As this sounded tedious to my callow sixteen-year-old mind, I got up to leave. A tall, slim man in his forties clad in faded denim took the stage, his flowing dark hair and beard lending him a messianic aspect. This was Brian Medlin, Professor of Philosophy. I sat down to listen, and the direction of my life changed.

I decided to check out this Flinders place, a new university in the suburbs, and on the library steps I encountered my second member of the faculty: this time a man clad entirely in black leather, his shaven head buffed to exceptional brilliance (with turtle oil, as legend had it). Enquiries revealed this to be a lecturer in Drama. Since I had to choose another Humanities subject to chime with the English and French courses I was committed to, Drama seemed to offer an interesting option. Read a few plays and that would be that, I thought.

It wasn't so simple. Drama was in fact the great talent magnet of the day, throwing me into the company of the bright, the provocative, the gifted, the outrageous, and the doomed who had come from far and wide, equipped with what passed for worldly experience to my teen mind. The stimulus of that company remains with me today, in ways both intangible and very direct as well: thirty-three years on, my wife Kerry and I (two children later) are still together – we met on those same library steps.

The world of film I stumbled into then has morphed over time into a 'career' (if we set aside the famous dictionary definition of career as 'a headlong rush, usually downhill'). Along the way, my crucial choices have had one final resource to rely on: instinct. Sure, the accidents of time and place have huge bearing on what Dickens calls the 'fragile daisy-chain' of our existence, but opportunity I believe knocks for most of us. What's important is: are you ready to hear it, have you equipped yourself to seize it and are you prepared to make it your own?

In 1986, instinct was to lead me to a little hall in Adelaide where I watched a pianist called David Helfgott take the stage in front of about a hundred people. Ten years later I came across an article about *Shine* in *Time* magazine which opened with the following sentence : 'David Helfgott, arguably the most famous pianist in the world . . . '! What an arc that story had – and what would've happened to me, to the Helfgotts, to Geoffrey Rush and numerous others if I'd kept the dinner engagement originally planned for that night instead of breaking it to go to this obscure recital?

'Follow your bliss' says Joseph Campbell. Listen to your own instinct. In the end, I believe the rhythm of your own drumbeat is the only one worth following.

ELIZABETH HONEY

Elizabeth Honey writes and illustrates for children. She grew up on a farm in Gippsland, and, after a circus came to Wonthaggi, she wanted to be a trapeze artist. But life took a different tack. She attended Morongo PGC Geelong, then studied film and television at Swinburne in Melbourne. After many years illustrating other people's stories she began to write her own.

A veteran of hundreds of school visits, Elizabeth's work includes picture books *Not a Nibble!* and *The Cherry Dress*, poetry *Honey Sandwich* and *Mongrel Doggerel*, and novels *Don't Pat the Wombat!*, *45 + 47 Stella Street*, *Remote Man* and *The Ballad of Cauldron Bay*, all published by Allen and Unwin.

Elizabeth cares very much for the environment, a theme woven into her stories. Her motto is 'No junk' and if that fails 'Disposal with honour'.

She feels the following would be best illustrated by two books of photographs: *The Family of Man* collected by Edward Steichen, and *The Family of Children* by Jerry Mason.

Somehow, by extraordinary chance, both you and
   I are humans.
What are the odds of this?
In the whole inconceivable cosmos is our small
   blue planet the only one with life?
As far as we know.

And on this Earth with its infinite variety are we a
    tree or a periwinkle?
No. From our fathers' zillion sperm and mothers'
    eggs I am me and you are you.
(What if another sperm had got there first?)
We hit the jackpot of life.
A babe urgently demanding, in our mother's arms
    we grow
and take it for granted.

How good it is to have a body.
What an apparatus! What an orchestration!
Senses neatly ranged on this commanding belfry
    co-ordinate the limbs.
We face each other, embrace each other.
No single bellbird note for us. We sing whole
    dictionaries.
We open our eyes and the world rushes in.
Peaches and strawberries, boronia, eucalyptus,
the sun on our backs and our toes in the river.
And a mind so plumb busy laughing and
    remembering and finding out.

It's the nature of human nature that's the worry.
Oh, we are commendable: kind, hardworking,
    ingenious, tolerant,
(cruel, lazy, thick, narrow).
But we humans, we want to be better. We humans,
    we always want more.
(Does everything have to be *owned*? Did the
    Aborigines want more?)

And some of this wanting is good: penicillin.
And some of this wanting is bad: the bomb.

We've reached a time when people have money.
Food on the table, a roof over our head.
We want the best for our children. We want the
    best for our children.
But the best things in life are free. Why bother
    with the old school tie?
But something for nothing is nothing. We *do* want
    our children to do well.

Real life is first hand do–it–yourself living.
Making, baking, give and taking.
Pop in for a snifter with Kerry and Old Dan.
No, he's not a boogyman, he's old as Methuselah.
You sing him off to sleep now, sing him off to
    sleep.
A patch of dirt, a cow, a crow, a daffodilly muddle,
a dance, a dare, a fish, a fire and ice upon a
    puddle.
And good old Mother Nature in her knobby club
    rush knickers ho ho he he HA HA HA!
Mucking around and all forms of dreaming. That's
    real life.

Second–hand life is pre–chewed.
TV teaches how to want, and to measure yourself
    by the stuff they have
(*Harry Potter*, the trophy book).
Don't buy into it.

TV stars the famously famous, famous for their
    fame, trailing courtiers of exquisite bitchiness.
Oh, there's good stuff on TV all right, but the
    electronic babysitter steals time;
that lively sly pickpocket slips it away while you're
    looking him square in the eye.
And growing bodies ripe for fun sit still.
Safe?

Meanwhile in other rooms
millions of electronic enemies are killed every
    second all around the world
by an army of solitary mercenaries in darkness.
The new war without casualties?
Pandora's laptop.
'Material' once hidden deep now blows about like
    autumn leaves.
Who downloaded this bestiality? What's his
    motive?

The Thought Police scramble to make new rules.
Does it matter?
We'll be jaded, but we'll think of something new.
Skimming skimming skimming skimming
Boy goes to stay with relatives at the beach. In the
    bedroom there were only beds.
Boy bored. Boy goes home three days early.

Yes, let's have awards for untidy towns.
We'll hike down from the mountain to the beach.
    (If they don't know the bush will they care

about it? If they never drink tap water will they
care about it?)

NASA shot a description of humans and our
address into outer space.
(They didn't tell *us* about this invitation!)
I'm afraid when the visitors show up our first
questions will be 'Are we better than them?
What can we get from them?' And we will want to
be in control.

In the meantime we'll continue to practise the
balancing act.
Hang on to real life.
Crack eggs and make glorious omelettes.
And when the time is right tell the dear young to
set sail. Go and see how other folk get by. Make
friends. Be cold and hungry, tired and broke, lost
and alone.
Go and find out who you are.
For one day soon you'll be in charge.

MARGARET JACKSON

Margaret Jackson is Chairman of Qantas Airways Limited. She became a Director of Qantas in 1992, and was appointed Chairman in August 2000. A full-time company director since 1992, Margaret Jackson is currently on the boards of ANZ Banking Group Limited, Billabong International and Southcorp Limited. She is also a member of the Foreign Affairs Council and Co-Chair of their Australia-New Zealand Leadership Forum.

A graduate of Monash University (B Ec) and Melbourne University (MBA), Margaret has had an extensive career with major firms Price Waterhouse, BDO Nelson Parkhill and KPMG. Margaret received an Honorary Doctorate in Laws from Monash University in 2002 and a Companion of the Order of Australia in the General Division (AC) in 2003.

Margaret's community interests lie in education – she is Chairperson of Melbourne Methodist Ladies' College – and in health, where she is a Director of the Howard Florey Institute of Experimental Physiology and Medicine, and is a former Director of the Brain Research Institute.

I am a working woman, and work is important to me. There's honour in work, and there's tremendous satisfaction in professional achievement.

But work is not the only thing in my life; indeed, it's not the most important thing. Prior to all else,

I am a daughter, sister, wife, mother and friend. And when I come to work, I bring these aspects of my life along with me. They inform who I am and what I believe – as well as how I do business.

Working life is far more about people and relationships and far less about technical information and know-how than the management gurus like to tell us. We all commence our careers with a set of technical or professional qualifications and skills. But the difference between professional success and failure largely depends upon how we relate to other people. The business leaders I admire are astute judges of character. They know how to motivate, communicate and collaborate with others to achieve results.

But to me, a successful life cannot be judged on work alone. Work ebbs and flows, but family and friendships are lifelong. The people you love are a source of strength and a reference point by which you can gauge where you are and where you should go next. They are the place where you can be accepted as yourself – and trusted, cherished and forgiven, no matter what.

I've seen very successful business people forget that they have lives beyond work. Work becomes their reason for living; as a consequence they put the rest of their life on hold. They downgrade family life; they neglect old friendships. And paradoxically, as a result of this, their work suffers. More importantly, when the work ends, as it must, they find themselves lost and alone.

Over the last several years two good friends of

mine have died suddenly. Life was over, far too soon. Like all those who loved them, I was devastated. I still miss them and grieve for them.

But something more than sorrow emerges from loss. I realised again just how brief a time we have on this earth. I was reminded again that life is precious, and far too short to defer happiness.

In this modern world we can get very hung up on failure. We can focus on what we can't do, not on what we might achieve. I have seen young people who hesitate to reach for their dreams. And older people who never make the big push for success. All because they are afraid they won't make it. They are afraid of being labelled a failure.

I would like to see an Australia where people reach with confidence and joy for their highest goals. I believe we must encourage our children to aim for the top – and to remember there's pride in trying, there's joy in every personal best performance, and there's no shame in being second best. Let's encourage those we love to live life to the full, and to cherish every moment.

Most of all, let's remember that who we are comes before what we do. Our relationships, our friendships, our connections within and across communities – these are what make life worth living. I hope to end my days with no regrets, knowing that I gave it my best shot. I am proud of my achievements as a working woman. But far, far more important to me are the quality of the relationships I sustain as a daughter, sister, wife, mother, and friend.

PETER JENSEN

Dr Peter F Jensen, Anglican Archbishop of Sydney, studied in Sydney at Moore Theological College, obtaining a B.D. from London University. He was subsequently awarded an M.A. degree by Sydney University, and earned his Doctorate of Philosophy at Oxford.

He has served in several positions in the diocese, notably as Principal of Moore Theological College for sixteen years. He has offered a significant contribution to the counsels of the Diocese of Sydney, and also to the national Anglican Church. He has written a number of books and other publications. In 2001 he was elected as Archbishop of Sydney, the largest diocese in this country.

He is married to Christine and they have five adult children and seven grandchildren.

As a Christian I know that I am supposed to believe that God is my heavenly Father and that he runs the world. The Bible says 'great is God's love towards us and the faithfulness of the Lord endures forever' (Psalm 117). That's what I am supposed to believe.

But there are times when this belief is sorely tested.

When our daughter, Elizabeth, told us she was pregnant we were, of course, delighted. This was our first grandchild. Two or three months later, however, there was some awful news. There were complications for the pregnancy and, as a result, the baby would not be able to survive outside the womb. We were devastated and, of course, shaken in our confidence in God our Father. How could this happen?

I still don't have a specific answer to that question. What we experienced in the next months, however, did re-affirm our trust in the faithfulness and goodness of God. It was not that he shielded us from the awful consequences of life in this world. It was not that he explained all that he was doing. But we could see that as we continued to try to walk in his ways, he blessed us with his presence and help.

Elizabeth decided to continue the pregnancy. She and her husband, Chris, said that they would give little Jonathan – they knew his name by now – the best life he could have. They were immensely brave and when Jonathan was born they, and the hospital, encouraged us to come and see him, to hold him, and to recognise that as short as his life had been he was, in fact, part of our family. In all of this, the hospital's practices and personnel were terrific. We found ourselves thanking God our Father for the way in which the hospital had helped us.

We had a proper funeral and that, too, was a marvellous, unforgettable day. The church was full of people. Once more, Beth and Chris were extraordinarily brave and full of faith. They could not answer the question of why this had happened – except, of course, that this is a world in which such tragedies occur. It has something to do with the way in which we human beings as a race have chosen to follow our own ways rather than the ways of God. Apart from that, the 'why?' question was beyond us.

But they did find that, rather than turning away from God, their instinct was to turn to God. They found they could trust God in and through the awful circumstances of grief, loss and death. Of course, it really helped to know that Jesus, the Son of God, also suffered terribly, and the resurrection of Jesus filled us all with hope.

At the grave-side there were about fifty friends and family. We sang a song called 'What a friend we have in Jesus, all our sins and griefs to bear'. It was an extraordinary moment as we realised that, since Jonathan had gone to be with Jesus, we would one day meet him. Elizabeth and Chris now have four other healthy children but, like them, we have never forgotten Jonathan, their first and our first. His death tested our faith in God, but also confirmed it. Sometimes we go to his grave and there on the small gravestone are the great words from Psalm 117: 'For great is God's love towards us and the faithfulness of the Lord endures forever'. All this I truly believe!

ALISON JOHNSON

Alison Johnson is a Sydney naturopath and is the Dean of the Australasian College of Natural Therapies, a position she has held for the past sixteen-and-a-half years. She is passionate about the growth and acceptance of Natural Medicine, and the education of its practitioners. She has a grown up daughter and son and a dog.

I believe in beauty
Beautiful things such as cathedrals, gardens, flowers and trees all uplift the spirits and allow us time to contemplate the world in a different and better way. Take the time to dwell on higher matters, to allow yourself to be lifted out of the humdrum and soothe your spirit.

I believe in humour
See the funny side of things, have some time each day when you can share a good laugh at the sheer absurdity of life. A smile and a laugh with someone will leave both of you feeling the better for the experience.

I believe in perspective
Assessing what troubles you in a very honest way allows you to see the path forward to changing

things. Even when the going is tough a bit of the Pollyanna principle lets us see that things really could be a lot worse.

I believe in empathy

Listening with an open heart as well as an open ear, giving someone your undivided attention, making the effort to understand in a non-judgmental way just how it is for another human being, not invalidating their experience by judging it by your own, and hearing what they have to say, is one of the greatest gifts we can give to another person. Try to give it often.

I believe in children

The world of children is a brief and magical place. To spend time back in the world of wonder and innocence is beautiful. Children have a way of cutting away the superficial in our daily lives and showing us what is really meaningful and important. Having children is important too. Seeing your child grow into a mature adult with children of their own is to see and understand the cycles of life. All those thousands of ancestors whose genetic material went to make you the unique person you are . . . Have you ever thought that if you don't have children, the line will end with you?!

I believe in dogs and cats and other pets
The de-stressing value of pets, the devoted love and enthusiasm of a dog, the joy a dog displays when you come home, these are things to be valued highly. Having a pet to talk to means you can talk to yourself without appearing too batty. A purring cat on your lap at night to stroke is very soothing and cosy.

I believe in company
Spending time talking to people of all ages, listening to their views just for the interest that is to be found in diversity. Time spent on a leisurely evening or Sunday afternoon with friends talking about anything and nothing, just going wherever the conversation takes you, covering as big a range of topics as you possibly can. The pleasure that can be gained by not having to prove your point, when just having a point is enough.

I believe in opinions
A great pleasure in life is there for us if we can enjoy listening to the opinions of others without feeling our life is threatened by an opposing point of view. Hearing a range of opinions opens us up to the possibility that we may possibly change our own.

I believe in good food
Having a healthy diet does not mean you don't eat delicious things. You can, you do, and you should.

Food shared is a great way to spend time with your friends and family. It provides a time for talk, a time for nurture, relaxation, a time to re-connect.

I believe in cooking

We should all be able to put together something tasty to eat. To be unable to cook means we are dependent on others for our very sustenance, and the others on whom we depend may not have our best interests at heart. To provide for our own is empowering.

I believe in living

We must live until we die, not sicken until we die. Take care of your health, your emotions, your spiritual growth and keep your sense of decency and dignity.

WILLIAM JONAS

Dr William Jonas is a Worimi man from the Karuah River area of New South Wales. He has been Aboriginal and Torres Strait Islander Social Justice Commissioner with the Human Rights and Equal Opportunity Commission since 1999. He was previously Director of the National Museum of Australia and Principal of the Australian Institute of Aboriginal and Torres Strait Islander Studies. He has held academic positions in Australia and overseas. In 1993 he was made a Member of the Order of Australia for his contribution to preserving Aboriginal culture and heritage.

Two people who had a very profound effect on my childhood and upbringing were my Uncle Dick and my grandmother, or Nana as we called her. Their influence strongly shaped what I believe today.

Uncle Dick was a wise, elderly Aboriginal man who had lived all of his life on his traditional country in the Karuah River Valley in New South Wales. This part of the river was a wide estuary so his land embraced both freshwater and saltwater country, the river flats and the wooded bordering hills. As a child he walked with me over all of this land, pointing out the beautiful, the revered, the feared and what was to be avoided. Many of the times we walked together in search of food.

One of the things which Uncle Dick always stressed was that we should never take more than we needed. Often, when I was really enjoying the fun of catching freshwater yabbies, or delighting in the thrill of landing fighting perch when they were in abundance, and I would beg to stay just a little bit longer and catch 'just another one', he would kindly steer me towards home. To this day I do believe that we have limited needs and that when we have enough to satisfy these we do not need to seek more.

My walks with my uncle were educational even though I didn't always realise this at the time. But by teaching me how to care for our environment my uncle showed me how we live in an interconnected world. I learned that if we polluted one part of the river then this would affect the quality of other parts of it. I learned that if we unnecessarily cut down trees and shrubs we could cause rapid soil erosion. I very strongly believe in this environmental interconnectedness. It is perhaps one of the reasons that I became a geographer but it also strongly influences my actions in the natural, urban, political, social, economic and other worlds in which I live.

Interestingly enough, my Nana taught me to believe in some similar things but from a very different perspective. Nana was a true English rose – beautiful, elegant, very pale and, like my uncle (her brother-in-law) very learned, experienced and wise. She was also very courageous, having married my grandfather in England prior to World War I before following him out to Australia to live with his family in the bush.

Despite her struggles and hardships, Nana seemed always to be happy. She enjoyed cooking for her children, grandchildren and friends and there was always laughter in her house. Christmas and birthdays were times of great celebration and cheer and the smallest amount of food could be turned into a feast. One day when I was at University and Nana and I were sharing a lunch, something we did when she occasionally came down to the big city for some shopping, she said to me quite clearly what I was beginning to believe. Her philosophy was to be happy, without making other people unhappy and without storing up unhappiness for the future. This loveliest and most-loved woman was a perfect proof of how this approach to life works and my belief in this philosophy has now guided me through many years. I guess, too, that my belief in the interconnectedness of our environment is strengthened by my Nana's approach and so I now also very strongly believe that there is an essential interconnectivity of time as well as of place.

ADIB KHAN

Adib Khan was born in Dhaka, Bangladesh. In 1973 he came to Australia where he completed a Masters Degree in English Literature at Monash University. Khan's first novel, *Seasonal Adjustments*, won the Christina Stead Prize for fiction and the Book of the Year in the 1994 New South Wales Premier's Prize, and won the 1995 Commonwealth Writers' Prize for First Book. He has written three other novels, his latest being *Homecoming* which was published in November 2003. Khan lives and teaches in Ballarat on weekdays and spends his weekends in Melbourne.

I am not among those who believe in the definitive pronouncement that the world has changed radically since September 11, 2001. Such a belief is arrogant in its assumption that the world only consists of the developed nations and a handful of countries that either harbour terrorists or have been directly affected by violence. How have things changed for the millions of villagers in Bangladesh? The peasant population of China? The inhabitants of Mongolia and Siberia? The rural communities in India?

What I do believe is that the complacency of the rich and powerful nations has been badly shaken. They no longer feel invincible. For much of the twentieth century, the developed countries of the world managed to create microcosms of self-sufficiency and live within their well-defined boundaries of prosperity. But such insularity also kills curiosity and generates ignorance. And ignorance leads to simplistic solutions whenever there is a problem that is perceived to be a significant threat to one's well-being. We need to look no further than the current situation in Afghanistan and Iraq.

The mentality of feudalism has lingered centuries after the structure itself has ended. Whatever may be the global state of affairs (and I am a firm believer in The Uncertainty Principle, which propounds the view that truth is not grounded in any form of absolutism but is entirely determined by perspectives), I feel that we are in a transitional phase in which the less affluent people of the world are no longer prepared to be bullied.

Terrorism is not only a matter of extreme ideology but is often the result of sheer desperation. What, I often ask myself, goes through the mind of a suicide bomber just before an explosive is detonated? What did Mohammad Atta and his accomplices feel as their plane was about to hit the tower? Was there regret? Panic? Fear? Or did their illusions of Paradise make them triumphant and fuel their determination to seek a perverse form of revenge on those they held responsible for the injustices in the Middle East?

There is no defence against those who are willing to self-destruct for the cause of perpetrating violence in the name of religion. Islam is not the only victim.

The activities of the Ku Klux Klan have been based on a distorted interpretation of Christianity, and the number of websites trumpeting Aryan superiority and the hatred of Jews, Africans and Asians is a chilling testimony of how the darkness of the mind and heart breeds evil. Recently we have the example of the American General Boykin, addressing a Christian prayer group with the claim that 'the enemy is a guy named Satan'. Such forms of fundamentalism raise questions about educational systems and their roles in developing human values and systems of belief.

The long-term counter measure to such problems is not force but secular education. The human spirit needs to be nourished, not brutalised. Humanism has to regain its status and be at the forefront of learning. The business world's greed for profitability, and technology's savage assault on ordinary lives, are carving a hollow at the centre of humanity. In growing numbers we seek spirituality and enlightenment, and yet we allow ourselves to be enmeshed in consumerism. Building ideals of success in materialism is merely suggestive of shallowness in our aspirations.

Evolution has not geared us for such rapid changes in our lives. We have to make a conscious effort to slow down. We need more time to discuss and reflect on what we are doing to the planet and to ourselves. Each of us bears a responsibility as a global citizen. Yes, we are Australians, Americans, Israelis and Palestinians, Christians, Hindus, Jews and Muslims. By all means let us celebrate our cultural identities. But we must never forget that, above everything else, we are humans – the supreme entities of this planet. It is time we started behaving with the wisdom and dignity befitting the custodians of our collective history with its monumental achievements and titanic blunders.

This I truly believe.

JONATHAN KING

Dr Jonathan King's beliefs were shaped by 'the school of hard knocks' – especially jackarooing and journalism, insights on the road, and some book learnin'.

On his paternal side, he inherited NSW third governor Philip Gidley King's traditions, with Scottish Highland humour on his maternal side. After failing English at Geelong Grammar, he worked outback in search of Banjo Paterson, then as a newspaper and television reporter in search of Superman's alias Clark Kent.

Organising mind-opening anti-Vietnam demonstrations he gained insights from Sociology at the London School of Economics and his English bride Jane (nee Lewis), before teaching politics at Melbourne University. He then learned from history's greats, organising and sailing on the 1988 bicentennial London to Sydney First Fleet re-enactment expedition; Bligh's *Bounty* voyage; Columbus's discovery of America; Marco Polo's voyage; Paterson's 'Waltzing Matilda' and 'Man from Snowy River' legends; Mary and Joseph's biblical Nazareth to Bethlehem journey; Matthew Flinders' Australian circumnavigation and Shackleton's Antarctic voyage – in short *Dancing with History*, the title of his forthcoming autobiography.

This above all, to thine own self be true;
And it must follow as the night the day
Thou canst not then be false to any man.

Polonius, Act 1, Scene 111,
Hamlet, Prince of Denmark, William Shakespeare.

Most westerners can achieve the first four of twentieth Century American psychologist Abraham Maslow's five 'needs' in his archetypical hierarchy: survival, security, sustenance and society; leaving us free to pursue self-actualisation – which I believe we have a duty to strive for.

Accordingly I believe our duties are to pair with the opposite sex in a loving monogamous relationship, reproduce the species, provide a long-term loving home for our offspring, sustain them till they fly the nest, and also give and take constructively from society. When it comes to tackling self-actualisation I agree with the epitaph I saw during an Antarctic expedition in 2003 on the tombstone of explorer Ernest Shackleton, in Grytviken, South Georgia: 'I hold that a man should strive to the uttermost for his life's set prize'. As a Christian this confirmed my long held belief in Victorian poet Robert Browning's adage, 'A man's reach must exceed his grasp, or what's a heaven for?' Both assumed a life's purpose that leaves the world a better place, rather than one spent getting rich quick serving a corporate giant or government bureaucracy.

But to find this life's purpose you must first find your true self and then stand fast. This gives you a rock foundation from which to achieve it. Just as you can't choose who you fall in love with, you can't always choose your life's purpose. It may take a while to find, but having chiselled out your personal self, this purpose should come to you if you nourish your instincts, intuition and sense of what is the real 'you' as against the socially conditioned 'you', identified by twentieth Century American sociologist Irving Goffman in *Presentation of Self in Everyday Life*. Be warned that most people never wake up to a self separate to society's needs for them to serve the system – never become aware that their socialisation has insidiously created 'the one dimensional man' identified by twentieth Century American socialist Herbert Marcuse.

Once this realisation of self and life's purpose comes, let go, take risks. Follow your heart. Cast off on your mission, passionately giving yourself to a greater cause, inevitably taking you to a higher sphere – which is what history's greats have done.

Unplanned, and directed by an unseen puppeteer, after discovering the tombstone of my ancestor Governor King in old England, my life's purpose has been bringing history to life telling didactic stories by producing re-enactments, films, books, articles and lectures. Dancing with history I have tried to share my life with inspiring partners (who strove *their* uttermost to achieve their life's purpose) by re-enacting their expeditions – Marco Polo (first to China), Christopher Columbus (first to America), Captain Arthur Phillip and his colleague and my ancestor Philip

Gidley King (who delivered the First Fleet to Australia, which I re-enacted in 1988), Captain William Bligh who survived the mutiny on the *Bounty* (the replica of which I helped buy for Australia) and Matthew Flinders (first to circumnavigate Australia). I have also honoured those who helped forge culture – Banjo Paterson ('The Man from Snowy River' and 'Waltzing Matilda', of which I organised Centenary celebrations in 1995), working with Elyne Mitchell ('Silver Brumby'), R.M. Williams (Stockman's Hall of Fame) and Slim Dusty; mentors one and all.

Giving their lives over to passions, and pulled along by an unseen force, they were tapped on the shoulder by causes far greater than themselves. Thus, along with Shakespeare's Hamlet, I believe 'there is a divinity that shapes our ends, rough-hew them how we will' and *feel* this is part of a spiritual dimension that has informed humans for thousands of years, inspiring some of humanity's *greatest* endeavours (especially medieval cathedrals) which is why I also commemorated the turn of the millennium by re-enacting the biblical journey of Mary and Joseph from Nazareth to Bethlehem.

Life itself on this beautiful planet with its sun, air, water and earth is such an environmental miracle that everyone has a duty to help preserve our heritage in their own way. But in the end if we are 'to our own self be true' we need to open our hearts and minds to the universe and then it should 'follow as the night the day' that we can give and get the most out of our blessed time on earth. This I believe.

MICHAEL KIRBY

The Hon Justice Michael Kirby, AC, CMG, is a judge of the High Court of Australia. For three decades he has been engaged in important legal, scientific and educational activities in Australia and beyond. He rose in the legal ranks from articled clerk to the High Court, stopping on the way for a time as a barrister and judge in various other courts. He has held judicial office for thirty years and is the longest serving man on the Australian Bench. He chaired the Australian Law Reform Commission when it was established. He also served on many international bodies. At the moment he is heavily engaged in the International Bioethics Committee of UNESCO. He is a public intellectual and that can sometimes be a dangerous thing in Australia.

I believe in rationality. It is the supreme and unique characteristic of our species. Together with love and empathy for others that grow out of rationality and our nature, it leads us on – pulling us away from our prejudices and irrational fears.

Look at the amazing times we live in. If the first judges who were sworn into office in the High Court of Australia in 1903 could come back, they would find, within the courtroom, much that was familiar. Yet once they stepped beyond the court door, they would be astonished. Fast cars. Aeroplanes in great number. Computers and the Internet. The world of the human genome. Laser technology, and, most fearsome of all, the power of nuclear fission. The exploration of outer-space. The images of human beings on the moon. The examination of the deep oceans. The coming world of artificial intelligence. The fantastic knowledge we now have about people everywhere. Satellite television that brings us brilliant sporting triumphs, wars from the other side of the world and tragedies closer to home.

How have these changes come about in the course of a century? Ironically, some of them are responses to terrible irrationality. The need to finish off World War II and defeat the fascists led to the Manhattan Project and the creation of nuclear weapons. The need to deliver those weapons by fast rockets produced the potential to explore space. This presented the necessity for miniaturisation so that the rockets could carry their payloads. This led, in turn, to the computer. This led, in its turn, to the capacity to map the genome. Everything, you see, is inter-connected.

So out of crazy irrationality has developed a remarkable world of science and technology. It contains the products of rational thinking. Human intelligence has also recognised the need for human cooperation. To bring peace and security to the planet. To promote greater economic equity. To defend individual human rights. Without cooperation, we might blow ourselves up or irradiate our world, destroying all forms of life, leaving everything to the cockroaches or microbes to start the story once again. Just as the world's previous dominant species, the dinosaurs, were destroyed, leaving the field to humans with their added capacity for conscious rationality.

This is why we need the United Nations. Annoying and inefficient as it can sometimes be, the United Nations is our best hope for global cooperation. It is why we now need international law. It is why we must defend human rights everywhere.

At the moment, the world is going through a dangerous irrational phase. Rationality and temperate values in matters of belief are under challenge. They are contested by terrorists and by doctrinaire absolutists in every land. At the heart of many of these challenges lies not, as such, a difference between Islam and other religions. The deep fault line of contemporary civilisations is found in attitudes to gender, sexuality and human diversity. There are some who cannot abide the idea of change in these respects. Typically, they are enemies of rationality. They deny science. They are contemptuous of knowledge and enlightenment. They are profoundly suspicious of technology. They do not see that rationality is the instrument given to human beings to expand their insight, increase their understanding and promote love and respect for diversity.

Out of our rationality, humanity has studied sexual diversity. Science has revealed the truth. For example, it is nature, not an evil passion, that has made some people homosexual. In the battle between misreadings of holy texts and the discoveries of science, rationality will always win in the end. So it did against the old belief that the earth was the centre of the universe. Or that the world was created in seven days. Or that slavery was morally neutral. Or that people of colour were the progeny of God's wrath towards man.

I believe in rationality because it shines a light of scientific truth on our world and on our species. We can bear the truth. It will set us free. Free from irrational hate and exclusion. Free to love our fellow human beings for what we are, in all of our diversity. The river of rationality is unstoppable. We are genetically programmed to quest for its healing waters. If we heed the rational mind we will save the species, build a better world, defend our environment and respect and love one another. Exclusion of difference is not the answer. Inclusion, harmony and love chart the way ahead. Irrationality is the enemy. Rationality is our better nature.

FRANÇOIS KLAUS

French-born François Klaus has been Artistic Director and Chief Choreographer of Queensland Ballet since 1998 and an Australian citizen since 2001. Following an extensive career in Europe as principal male dancer with the prestigious Hamburg Ballet, he spent six years in Switzerland as Artistic Director of Bern State Ballet and subsequently of Ballett Art. He has created more than fifty ballets, his work being recognised in Switzerland by the Doron Cultural Prize in 1996 and, since his arrival in Australia, by a nomination for a Helpmann Award. He also received a Centenary Medal for distinguished service to the arts.

I believe that dogs can smile.
I believe especially in the smile of a French
    bulldog.
It convinces me that goodness is a reality.

I believe that tulips are beautiful.
But they thrive in the cold, wet weather of Spring.
Does this mean that perfection is an elusive
    coincidence?

Science tells us that the universe is a purely
    material creation.
Are we just a material consequence?

If so, why should matter look at itself?
Could it be that awareness created matter?

Why are so many things actually harmonious?
I liked to listen to music while observing plankton
    under a microscope.
With the music of Bach, it created perfect
    harmony.

Why are efficient machines often beautiful?
Is it not a little sad that a beautiful chord is just a
    number of vibrations?

Is a mathematical formula a recipe for beauty?
Could it be that our most intimate feelings
Somehow correspond to a mathematical logic?
Does it mean that the divine and structure are one
    and the same?

I believe in a French bulldog's smile.
It is such a comforting thought.

PHILLIPE KLAUS

Born in Hamburg (Germany) to French/Australian parents, Phil is fifteen years old. His family moved to Bern in Switzerland when he was two and he attended a Swiss school before moving to Brisbane at the age of nine. Phil currently attends The Gap State High School, where he has been recognised regularly for academic excellence. He has been playing piano and composing since an early age and in 2003 his composition *Nereid* was selected for an award in the Keys National Piano Competition. Phil enjoys many activities, especially those associated with the performing arts. He has a particular passion for music and drama.

If someone asked me to make a list of all the things I can say I honestly believe in, it would be very short. This is mainly because my beliefs change constantly. Whenever I feel I have a clever opinion on something, I often find myself being exposed to a different point of view and suddenly, I'm not so sure. At fifteen, I think it's all right not to be absolutely sure of your opinions. I guess right from when I was small, even the simplest things, like names, weren't straightforward. For some people, a cat has always been a cat. For me, a cat was called a *cat* at home, a *katze* at school and *un chat* by my grandmother. People say that broadens the mind, but maybe it also makes you more unsure.

Nevertheless, the big ideas like light and dark, right and wrong, seem very real concepts to me. Your interpretation of these concepts governs your life. It's when you get down to defining them that things get difficult. A long time ago, I used to believe there was a definite line between right and wrong. Some things were good, some bad. Then I discovered those things which seemed to fit into both categories at the same time, hence my definite line got very shaky. I reckon religion is a good example. So many people have been helped, both spiritually and practically, by devout religious practitioners. On the other hand, the name of religion has been behind so many atrocities. In fact, there's a good and bad side to everything I know, which makes long-lasting beliefs even harder to form.

However, trying to think about a few things I really believe in, I thought about a couple of things I *don't* believe, at least at the moment. I don't believe that the media in general do their best to inform people about the different aspects of a situation or event. It seems there's an awful lot of talking down to people. We can't grow up to be a race of thinking people if we're not given anything to think about. Similarly, I try not to believe too much of what I hear from politicians. They seem to try to control rather than represent the people, and never seem to simply answer questions in interviews.

It's often hard to define why something is worth believing in. Along with others, I have a passion for music, but what is it that makes music so important? You can dribble on about pitch and harmonies as much as you want, but there's no escaping the fact that it's just a bunch of sounds. Yet for me there's something magical about music. Whatever you believe in, I guess there's something about it that makes it important to you and others like you but stays intangible to other people. So I believe it's important to respect other people's beliefs even if they stay obscure for you personally.

I *do* believe that you need belief. Without belief, there would be no going forward. Belief, though, is like a ship on the ocean. If you keep going forward in a straight line you'll eventually hit a rock. That's why it's often a good idea to sail in zigzags.

BEN KOZEL

In February 2000, Ben Kozel stood at the edge of the Atlantic Ocean, having rafted the entire length of the Amazon. In doing so he became a member of only the third team ever to successfully trace the world's biggest river from source to sea. In 2001, Ben and Colin Angus recruited Tim Cope (Young Australian Adventurer of the Year) and a Canadian friend for a journey along the fifth longest river in the world – the Yenisey. This river begins in Mongolia and travels 5,500 kilometres north through Siberia (nearly twice the size of Australia) until it reaches the Arctic Ocean. Using kayaks, a rubber raft and then a wooden boat, they became the first people to travel the full length of the Yenisey.

The resulting documentary of their journey, *Yenisey: River of Extremes* (award winner at the 2003 Banff Film Festival) has recently been purchased by the National Geographic Channel.

Since his return from Siberia, Ben has completed his science degree and is currently living in Adelaide where he is preparing for his next journey – this time to explore the Berber homelands in Saharan North Africa.

Ben has written two books: *Three Men in a Raft* was published in 2002, and *Five Months in a Leaky Boat* was published in 2003.

Fear and greed – they are two integral elements of the human condition that have arguably shaped our world more than any others. Though deriving from the 'kill, or be killed' ethos that dominated the prehistoric mindset, it could be argued that they are as manifestly evident today, in spite of our self-proclaimed civility and humanitarianism. That said I do not see fear and greed as inescapable burdens on humanity, but as conditions that can be transcended. Knowledge and awareness, together with a readiness to engage the unfamiliar, create a formidable force for peace, promote harmony between cultures and allow us to appreciate our dependence on a healthy environment. And only by being aware of and understanding what is out there can we appreciate what is at risk of being lost.

Modern cities have become a swaddle of cotton wool. Increasingly, the wilderness, the natural environment, has been relegated to something almost otherworldly. Recently, a friend of mine recounted how a little bird had caused near chaos when it started flying around her office. Most people do not think of the world beyond the swaddle. They visit the supermarket when they need food, without for an instant considering where that food came from. Of the few who do, even fewer consider that the goods we, as a society, now demand might be supplied by agricultural, manufacturing or refining processes that are not environmentally sustainable.

As a conservationist, my philosophy originally centred on the belief that I should push against that relentless juggernaut of 'unsustainable development', slowing it down ever so slightly, buying more time for the enlightenment of the masses, who would then halt that juggernaut before it carried us all into oblivion. It was a somewhat simplistic view. A far bigger, more complex picture emerged when I began to travel to regions in which live societies whose outlooks were fundamentally different from that of the society that raised me. I came to acutely realise that the health of the global environment is inextricably linked to cultural awareness, understanding and respect.

The reality is, however, that developing nations' resources are exploited either by bullying multinationals or else by governments desperately trying to repay their debts to the developed nations. In the process, human rights are trampled; entire proud cultures are left to starve. Yet even those who openly deplore it all suffer from ritual inaction, a scourge more devastating than any war or famine. And how else can you explain this sitting on hands except by invoking detachment – an inability to identify with the 'other'? Someone who has never lugged their drinking water 50 kilometres to their home finds it easy to leave the tap running while they brush their teeth. So too, those who have never known anything other than a stable democratic society can easily dismiss as maniacal others who are willing to lay down their life for political reform.

A recent survey conducted by National Geographic found that an alarming number of young

Americans could not even point to their own country on a map of the world. And while we'd like to assume that Australian youngsters couldn't possibly be bereft of such awareness, how many could point to Iraq if asked?

Ought we to be disturbed then by the trend for geography to disappear from the classroom? Can such apathy for learning about the world be blamed on an innate reluctance to look beyond our backyard? Or does it stem from not having our childhood passion for discovery sufficiently nurtured? It's fair to say that many of us switch off when information is presented in a fashion that does not encourage us to find some attachment between it and our view of the world. Furthermore, so much of what we do take in remains one-dimensional, intangible.

To my mind, we have an obligation to cultivate a connection between the young, the unborn, and the wealth of diversity offered by this earth they will inherit. Because if we can retain a child's sense of wonder, that thirst for discovery and capacity for open mindedness, then it's my belief that a good number of the injustices and horrors we tend to habitually take for granted will quickly recede to memory.

CARMEN LAWRENCE

After serving in the West Australian Parliament from 1986 and making history by becoming Premier of Western Australia and Australia's first woman Premier in February, 1990, Dr Carmen Lawrence was elected Federal Member for Fremantle in March, 1994. Soon after entering Federal Parliament, Dr Lawrence was appointed Minister for Human Services and Health Minister Assisting the Prime Minister for the Status of Women.

Since the defeat of the Keating Government in 1996, Dr Lawrence has held various shadow portfolios. On 14 November 2003, Dr Lawrence was elected by the first popular ballot of ALP members as President of the Australian Labor Party.

Dr Lawrence is an active and vocal peace campaigner, regularly speaking at rallies and forums around the country. Dr Lawrence also speaks and writes regularly about refugee policy and democratic reform.

One of the reasons I enrolled to study Psychology at the University of Western Australia as a raw convent girl of sixteen was my fascination with the question of how people come to hold the beliefs they do. I was curious about the formative influences and experiences on each individual's view of the world. I wondered what causes us to change our beliefs and whether we act in ways that are consistent with our belief systems. I was particularly interested in religious beliefs and political attitudes, in prejudice and its antithesis, open-mindedness.

Perhaps as a result of my education, I am passionately committed to the idea of equality – not that everyone is equally clever or attractive or articulate, but that each person has equal worth. As one of my '60s heroes (I was a child of the times), Robert Kennedy, put it:

> We must recognize the full human equality of all of our people before God, before the law, and in the councils of government. We must do this, not because it is economically advantageous, although it is; not because the laws of God command it, although they do; not because people in other lands wish it so. We must do it for the single and fundamental reason that it is the right thing to do.

Kennedy's views, like my own, owed a lot to the teachings of the Catholic Church which incorporate the injunction that we should all be treated as equal before God.

Although I am no longer a believer, I still heed Christ's admonition that we have an obligation to our fellow citizens and that we are all equally deserving, no matter who we are or where we come from. The nuns who taught me were in no doubt that we were obliged as Christians to treat everyone with respect and to do so out of love.

There is an explicit principle of equality in Christian theology. Paul, for example, says quite forthrightly that for Christians, 'There is neither Jew nor Greek, there is neither slave nor free, there is neither male nor female; for you are all one in Christ Jesus' (Gal. 3:28).

Because of this belief that all stand before God equally and all are equally creatures of God, an enlightened Christian society can hardly justify anything but a commitment to equality within its political framework.

As an aside, I find it disturbing that some of those who claim to be Christian and indeed pray before the Parliament meets every day for divine guidance are the very same people who talk about 'dole bludgers' and 'job snobs', who denigrate asylum seekers and show calculated disrespect to Indigenous people.

Christianity, of course, is not unique among religions in this recognition of the equal worth of all human beings. The other major religions share a similar commitment, and secular humanists and socialists promote a similar vision of society, without the theological reasoning.

The latter started from the premise, which I find compelling, that luck, rather than virtue, is one of the great determinants of life. H.G. Wells and his socialist friends began their influential Declaration of Rights with the observation that 'since a man comes into the world through no fault of his own' . . . and they might have added, 'and with no choice over where and in what circumstances' . . .

One of my abiding convictions is that the recognition of our equal worth compels us to act to break down inequality, to reduce disadvantage and suffering wherever it occurs, to eschew violence against our fellow human beings and to work to systematically break down limitations on people's achievement and their ability to share in society's goods. With recognition of the equal worth of human beings and the unequal distribution of power and privilege goes the obligation to use one's talents for the common good.

I can do no better than quote Robert Kennedy again who said, almost thirty-five years ago, to students at Berkeley:

> You can use your privilege and opportunity to seek purely private pleasure and gain. But, history will judge you, and as the years pass you will judge yourself, by the extent to which you have used your gifts to lighten and to enrich the lives of your fellow human beings. In your hands, not with presidents or leaders, is the future of your world and the fulfilment of the best qualities of your own spirit.

CHRISTOPHER LAWRENCE

Christopher Lawrence is a writer and broadcaster. The *Swoon Collection* CDs that evolved from his popular breakfast programme on ABC Classic FM (1994–98) have all achieved Platinum status and therefore help keep the peace in hundreds of thousands of homes. He has also been a guest conductor of all the Australian capital city symphony orchestras, much to their amusement.

His latest book is *Swing Symphony: Another midlife adventure in the south of France* (Random House Australia, November 2004). Christopher also writes for the international magazines *Opera* and *Opera Now*.

I began to talk very late. When I was three and a half my despairing parents took me to a specialist to try and discover what was wrong. It turned out that I was not suffering from any learning difficulties: I was just stubbornly mute. Reproducing tunes, not lyrics, was my forte. The family radiogram fell victim to my rough playing and replaying of our record collection of Broadway musicals, all of which I could then hum by rote. Negotiating the tricky intervals of Bernstein's *West Side Story* presented no problem to my infant ear, but Sondheim's marvellous words did not interest me in the slightest. Three-year-olds do not lose sleep over meeting girls called Maria.

Eventually my mouth split open and whole sentences gushed out. Not being content with having broken my silence, I proceeded over the ensuing forty years to make a living from talking into a microphone. There was at least a thread of continuity from childhood in that I was still playing records – now little shiny ones – and the 'talking' was mercifully concise; enthusiastic haiku-length labelling, enclosed by chunks of classical music. But words seduced me. I became enamoured of them and moved on to other radio shows in which talking was paramount. The shows were successful and I was always grateful that listeners seemed happy to have me talk to them. Their acceptance of this unequal discourse was a privilege.

One day I peered through the forest of my words all the way back to those first blissful years before the onset of eloquence. I admired my early discretion. It was, perhaps, the wisest period of my life; not being ignorant of speech, but seeing no good reason to resort to it when the option of listening was not only more fun, but more instructive.

This was a revelation. I still enjoyed my work, yet wondered sometimes if all I was doing was merely adding to the world's clamour. One day it became impossible to imagine what I would talk about for three hours that evening, having drained my mental reservoir of remembered fact long before. If there were a danger that I might make do with hastily contrived opinion, I would rather not talk at all; the world already had too much of it. Shortly after this I decided to stay away from microphones for a while. I would still play with words, but on paper.

So far it has been a good sabbatical. While I am not a Trappist, music and silence have been reinstated to what I believe to be their rightful place in my life. Together they leave room for thoughts to ripen, without being attached prematurely to the wheels of speech and dragged, flailing and ugly, into the open air.

This is doubtless a useless belief in a world addicted to the banalities of innumerable half-baked remarks, yet with all the authority of a student teacher in an anarchic schoolroom, I suggest that so much more might be possible if we could all just shut up for a while. That, and teach our three-year-olds to hum *West Side Story*.

Have I used too many words to say this? Probably.

HUGH MACKAY

Hugh Mackay is a psychologist, social researcher and novelist. He has made a lifelong study of the attitudes and behaviour of Australians and, since 1979, has been publishing his findings in the quarterly research series, *The Mackay Report*. He is the author of four bestsellers in the field of social psychology (*Reinventing Australia*, *The Good Listener*, *Generations* and *Turning Point*) and four novels (*Little Lies*, *House Guest*, *The Spin* and *Winter Close*). His latest book is *Right and Wrong: How to Decide for Yourself*.

I believe the most fundamental of all human needs is the need to be recognised as a unique individual. If you doubt it, look at what happens when people feel as if they are *not* being properly acknowledged: they become angry, stressed, cynical, aggressive or petulant – to say nothing of plain unhappy.

There's rarely a single, simple cause of unhappiness (or of its more brutal cousin, depression) but, somewhere in there, you'll usually find a person who feels under-valued, unappreciated or misunderstood. Not being taken seriously enough – by our partners, parents, friends, colleagues, politicians, or even by banks and other service providers – feels like a slap in the face.

Perhaps this is why so many people take *themselves*

so seriously: 'If no-one else will give me the recognition I deserve, I'll do the job myself.' So a good reason for giving sympathetic acknowledgement to other people – especially those closest to you – is that you might save them from the lonely descent into hubris.

I believe humans can best be understood as herd animals. Most people feel comfortable in herds (families, friendship circles, work-groups) of about seven or eight, and somewhat uncomfortable outside them. But our shrinking households are no longer robust enough to satisfy our herd instinct: in fact, half of Australia's households contain only one or two people. So now, to compensate, we enthusiastically attach ourselves to non-domestic herds – work-groups, cooking classes, book clubs, sporting associations, adult education courses. We graze with the herd in cafes and food courts; when all else fails, we herd electronically, via the Net or SMS.

Being herd animals, we feel most confident and secure when we have strong and visionary leaders. Weak or cynical leaders, or those who seem more interested in their own power than our well-being, make us feel uneasy, disengaged and powerless. Leadership vacuums tend to be filled either by demagogues or by our own unbridled self-interest.

I believe human nature is a complex blend of rational and non-rational impulses that can rarely be explained by logic. Our brains are awash with hormones (more like glands than computers); we do things we say we'll never do; we sometimes disapprove of our own actions but go ahead anyway. Our moral codes are subjective and flexible: even the Golden Rule, which many of us claim to embrace, is distorted, in practice, into something like 'treat other people the way you think they'd probably treat you' – a virtual contradiction of the original idea.

I've discovered that everyone's story is interesting: if you find someone boring, that just means you haven't got to know them well enough. I've also come to realise that everyone's story is tinged with sadness; happiness visits most of us but fleetingly, and that's okay. (Whoever said happiness was the only authentic emotion?)

I've learnt to despise intellectual arrogance, because it fails to acknowledge the genetic accident that makes some people less intelligent than others. I've learnt to be suspicious of people who've made a lot of money quickly: too often, it turns out they've cut moral corners, exploited others, charged uncon-scionable prices for their goods or services, or simply been devious in their business dealings.

Poverty is a blight on society, but I have the deepest respect for people who work long and hard and manage to live responsible, generous and fulfilling lives without ever achieving the kind of material prosperity rich people take for granted.

I believe the meaning of our lives is to be found in the quality of our personal relationships, and nowhere else. We are all part of the same humanity. We learn our most valuable lessons from each other.

FRANCIS MACNAB

Dr Francis Macnab is founder, and executive director, since 1961, of The Cairnmillar Institute – a centre for psychotherapy, professional training and community education. He has lectured widely in many countries and has written some twenty-five books.

He is also the executive minister of St Michael's Uniting Church, Collins Street, Melbourne – a church that strongly advocates rigorous ways in which psychology and religion can contribute to personal health and a more compassionate community.

He is a Fellow of the British and Australian Psychological Societies and also of the Australian College of Educators.

Her reddened eyelids showed she had been crying. She turned to introduce her three daughters. All of them were in their teens. They had come to talk through their distress. The man they loved – husband and father – had committed suicide. There had been no sign of his intention. No note to disclose his reason.

Said the mother, 'The stresses had got on top of him.' 'Why did he not tell us he was in some trouble?' asked one daughter rhetorically. 'He was always our model of strength,' said the second. And the third daughter seemed to say what they were all thinking – 'What are we to believe, when our own father throws his life away? What are we to believe?'

A knock on the door, a policeman's face in the darkness, and their world of goodness and expectation collapsed. Their belief in a father's strength suddenly became a devastating awareness of his vulnerability.

'The stresses were too much for him,' the mother repeated as if to comfort her daughters and blame some external cause for her husband's behaviour. She believed that stresses – whatever they are! – could kill. She believed that pointing to a cause could excuse. She believed that somewhere in this chaos there had to be some consolation.

The first daughter burst in and said, 'Why would he do such a terrible thing to us? Such a burden to carry! Surely no stress could outrun his concern and love for us! What are we to believe now? Was he sick? Was he out of his mind? Was he out of his depth? Why would he act so out of character? What are we to believe?' The questions flowed on.

We all sat in a silence that stretched beyond endurance. There were no answers.

The mother spoke: 'We can only believe in our own strength – the strength we each have and the strength we all have together. We have to believe in the strength to say: Now that this calamity has occurred, what is our best way to cope with it? We need to believe in the strength to pick ourselves up and not become life-time victims of our tragedy.'

'How can you sit there and say that?' asked the

second daughter. 'I've done nothing to deserve this. He always told us to be good, caring people. That's what he believed! Now all that's in tatters and you say we are to go on believing in something . . . What?'

The mother replied, 'We will never understand why life visits such harsh times on people. We can't claim any exemptions. If tragedy hits, we all have a choice: whether we will be blocked by what has happened, or whether we will get up and go on, determined to find the best way to go forward. I believe all four of us can help each other do that. I believe we will find a way through our worst nightmare.'

She was saying, 'These are things I believe':

I believe we are all exposed to unexpected and undeserved tragedy and chaos.

I believe we have the strength to ask, 'How will I cope with this in the best possible way?'

I believe in the strength people give to each other.

I believe that there is some consolation, even in our worst chaos.

I believe there is a strength in the faith we have in life, where hope sits alongside our difficulties and crucifixions await our resurrections.

The mother and her three daughters walked outside. I watched them through my window. They put their arms around each other, and stood in the sunshine for a time that seemed endless. I turned away, convinced of another belief:

I believe in the healing strength of silence.

This particular tragedy could have been any tragedy. A life-crisis can take many forms. Any tragedy can drain all sense of meaning from us. It can undermine that important belief in ourselves, our support groups, and the inspirational models and resources that would carry us into a different future. I believe there are positive transformative possibilities in the way we shape our future.

JOHN MARSDEN

John Marsden was born in Victoria, spent his childhood in Tasmania, his adolescence in New South Wales, and most of his adult years back in Victoria. He is the author of thirty-three books, mostly novels, and mostly for young people. These include *So Much to tell You*, *Letters from the Inside*, and the *Tomorrow* series. He has sold more than three million books world-wide and won major awards in Australia, Europe and the U.S.A. In 2004 he was described on ABC television as 'perhaps Australia's most influential author'.

I was on the train from Calgary to Vancouver. The mountains towered around us, lavishly covered with snow. Bears, elk, antelopes, deer, golden eagles, bald eagles were in abundance, along with little furry things running around in the undergrowth.

I wished I had bigger eyes, to take it all in.

At lunch on the first day I was seated opposite a retired Australian, from Wangaratta. In the course of conversation I said something about Japan. He leaned forward a little, smiled at me, and said 'Yes, but those Japanese . . . they all look alike, don't they?'

I choked on my bread roll but didn't attempt to answer.

We stayed overnight in a hotel, and resumed the journey the next day. After our stopover, the same man said to me 'They don't have the houses that we do, did you notice? We have better housing in Australia.'

A little later, as we stood on the observation platform looking at the vast lakes and forest, he said 'They don't have as many birds as we do. We've got more birds in Australia.'

I looked at him in disbelief. 'Have you been counting? Does it matter?' The idea that we were engaged in some sort of international competition had escaped me.

I thought briefly of pushing him under the wheels of the train.

On the way home I thought a lot more about him though.

It seems to me that we are all born in ignorance, but it's a good idea not to stay there. If there is a 'meaning of life' it won't be found unless we move a certain way from that starting point. And it's possible that the journey from ignorance to whatever-you-want-to-call-it (I call it awareness) is in itself the meaning of life.

People like Jesus, Mohammed, Buddha and others may have gone all the way – I'm fairly sure I'll never know whether that was true of them – but the rest of us are unlikely to travel so far. To move at all is good, to move a long way is remarkable.

When a person doesn't move it is always a tragedy. Such people are frustrating to deal with, as they are deaf to reason, impervious to emotional appeals, incapable of imagination. Conversations with them are often best avoided.

Unfortunately schools don't know anything about this stuff. They take students on a different journey, the one from ignorance to knowledge. That can be a journey worth taking, but it in no way resembles the one to awareness or wisdom. At worst it results in a person who can recite the names of every Wimbledon quarter finalist since 1908, at best in a person who can identify a rare illness and knows how to treat it.

In my own attempts to move towards awareness I haven't got very far. But I've figured out a few things that seem true to me. One is that people who have no meaningful roles and responsibilities in a society can become alienated, angry, depressed, or all of the above. As long as we continue to deny young people meaningful roles and responsibilities in schools and in the wider community, we can expect many of them to become unhappy and destructive . . . even self-destructive.

Another is that crime is illness. It is impossible for happy well-balanced, secure people who were treated with loving care as children to commit crimes. If we understood this we would change our treatment of 'criminals', starting this afternoon.

The third is that people who seek power should never be given it. Whether it's a job as Prime Minister or as Principal of a school or as leader of a group, the desire for power and the belief that one can take on such a responsibility is sure proof of megalomania. Res ipse loquitur. The thing speaks for itself.

We have a lot of work ahead of us in Australia. In their violations of the human rights of refugees, abuses carried out in our name, I think politicians have used public policy as a drunk might use a trench-digger in a garden. I see terrible gouges right across the country: deep and ugly scars. Words and phrases like 'fair go', 'mateship', and 'sticking up for the battlers' sound ludicrous now when used in the context of an Australian identity. I don't think we can ever use these words again, but we must do the best we can to repair what we can.

The journey continues. T. S. Eliot wrote 'We had the experience, but we missed the meaning.'

The man from Wangaratta had the experience of his train trip through Canada. But he might have been better off staying home and reading T. S. Eliot.

Bruce McAvaney

For more than twenty-five years Bruce McAvaney has been sitting in the box seat at some of the world's most exciting sporting events.

As a five-year-old living in the Adelaide suburb of Ferryden Park, his ambition was to call the Melbourne Cup, which he did – three times. He's also appeared on Australian television calling AFL Grand Finals, Athletics and Swimming World Championships, the Australian Open tennis and seven Olympic Games.

He's known as the bloke who never saw a statistic he didn't like – and he reckons he's the luckiest bloke in the world.

At the age of fifty, you tend to look back at your life and assess it: where you've come from, what you've learned, what the rest of your life holds for you.

There's a danger in defining yourself by what you do for a living but as luck would have it, what I do is what I love. If I were disabled tomorrow, I would still have the same interest in athleticism and sport that I did when I was five years old, pretending to call the Melbourne Cup.

That sounds contradictory, I know. But the performance of the human body – the ability of the mind to push the body to limits beyond the imagination – will never lose its fascination for me.

At the moment I'm preparing for the Olympic Games, so the Olympics are uppermost in my mind as they are every four years: the ultimate sporting event.

What makes it so?

My favourite Olympic appraisal is from writer Simon Barnes in the London *Times*. He says:

> The Olympic Games are something seriously special. Everywhere you look is the most important day of somebody's entire life. Nothing less. The World Cup? Forget it. Just thirty-two nations, one sport, and worst of all, one sex. The Olympic Games celebrate the biodiversity of human nature: giants, pixies, stars from every race, every belief. And women. A tale without women is half a tale.

Particularly true for me. Cathy Freeman provided me with the race of my broadcasting life, four years ago in Sydney.

But there were other Australians who sent a tingle up my spine while I was growing up: Herb Elliott's 1500 metres in Rome in 1960, when he won by 20 metres, broke his own world record, and became the first Australian male to win on the track for more than 60 years . . .

In Tokyo, Betty Cuthbert – the golden girl of 1956 – who retired after Rome, coming back to glory one more time in the 400 metres when she was supposedly well past her prime.

Her teammate in Tokyo, the irrepressible Dawn Fraser, whose preparation had been so compromised after she was injured in a car accident which killed her mother. In 1964, still unable to abide by the rules, Dawn became the only person, male or female, to win gold in the same swimming event – the 100 metres freestyle – in three consecutive games.

I was starting to see not just the achievements, but the journeys behind them. The stars of the festival were all flesh and blood. There's no easy road to the Olympics.

And so I looked for, and found, the stories behind the athletes; discovering each of them to be an incredible adventure – but more fascinating than fiction:

Dorando Pietri collapsing at the end of the marathon in London in 1980; decathlete Jim Thorpe excelling in Stockholm only to have his medals taken away for the crime of 'professionalism' – and then reinstated seventy years later; and the battle between Vladimir Kuts and Gordon Pirie in Melbourne over 10,000 metres. It set my heart pumping – and yes, my spirit soaring.

When your heroes are more aligned with your own age, the excitement is even greater . . . And with the arrival of television, we could *see* the saga unfolding.

I'd never have believed I'd witness first-hand the best of the best performing live – let alone have the chance to tell their stories to a wider audience.

Luck, and desire . . . so I have something in common with my Olympic heroes.

And the truth is, watching is not nearly as good as calling the action.

In 1984 I went to Los Angeles and watched Carl Lewis's debut: a superman capable of anything – he has nine gold medals. And there I saw Seb Coe create history, becoming the first man to win the 1500 metres twice. An unforgettable last lap: Ovett broken physically, Cram challenging and Coe running for his life.

Thousands of athletes at each Olympics; none of them treading an easy route to get there.

To Sydney: a magnificent Monday night with the majority of Australians, black and white, male and female, focussing on Cathy Freeman. One minute of her life, one lap around the stadium. It mattered to so many people.

That was a fairytale ending.

It could have turned out so differently, as it did for the thousands of other athletes who fell on the wrong side of that knife-edge between first and nowhere.

We human beings are social animals. We love to compare ourselves with others. We admire those we perceive to be better than we are. We look for, and find, heroes. We need them.

I find heroes in the sporting arena. Others find them in the arts, the great thinkers of our time, the great inventors.

These heroes are who we aspire to be. Unlike gods, they bleed, and we love them the more for it.

Don McIntyre

Don McIntyre has lived a life of adventure and continues to do so. Surfing, racing motorcross, building cars, parachuting, gliding, hunting, flying, scubadiving, sailing, fishing and building a successful business preceded his 1990–91 entry in the BOC Challenge Single-handed Around the World Yacht Race, a 26,000 mile, nine-month adventure that was eight years in the planning. He came second in his class in this event, which is considered the Everest of yachting. In 1996 Don and his wife, Margie, received the Australian Geographical Societies' highest honour by being awarded a gold medal as Adventurers of the Year, following an epic twelve months living together alone in a box, chained to rocks in Antarctica. Since then, he has been adventuring full-time in the tropics and Antarctica, sharing the experience with school children around the world. Most recently he has taken his 36-metre, helicopter-equipped ice ship, *Sir Hubert Wilkins*, to Antarctica and on a treasure-hunting expedition to the Philippines.

As an eleven-year-old boy I was shocked to the core when I discovered I only had two years to live. At that age your horizons are justifiably close. The big picture hasn't entered your head, apart from what you learn at Sunday school. But there it was in black and white on the pages of *Australasian Post* magazine . . . the world was doomed! A giant meteor would collide with Earth days before my thirteenth birth-day. I was going to die! The article was truly scary; overpowering the bikini clad women on the preced-ing pages.

I was bewildered and confused that this situation was out of my control – and worse, no one seemed to care! Why weren't people making preparations? Where were we going to hide? What could I do? Nothing, I was going to die. Discovering my own mortality was profound and now, thirty-eight years later, death is still indirectly the catalyst to a driving force greater than survival itself, and a partner to this essay. When you come to terms with the inevit-ability of death you appreciate and value the gift of a healthy life and the passion you must give it.

Having faced death as a little boy, my next awaken-ing came as a teenager, camping in the country on a clear night, lying on my back searching for satellites and falling stars. My consciousness began to race beyond the stars; how far to the furthestmost? What is beyond that? The black bits between aren't the ceiling of a room, so where does it end? How far out is for-ever? Where are the boundaries? I had real difficulties comprehending that space had no boundaries. If so, then, why should life? What am I? What are we? What's it all about? The big picture was intriguing and told me to live.

This book is loaded with diverse beliefs and I am sure, reading between the lines, many are similar, as we are all human beings on one earth exposed to life. When, where, how and with whom you are born sets the foundations of your exposure to life, but then it is up to you. I believe in many things . . . you make your own luck by meeting people and grabbing opportunities others don't perceive, or do and pass them up, and live with regret.

I believe you have to dream before you plan, so why not have big dreams? I believe being satisfied and content with what you have shouldn't stop you trying for the lot. I believe in having a go even if others say you shouldn't. I believe experience in anything is better than no experience at all, which brings me to flat-lining. This I believe dearly. If you get hot, on goes the air-conditioner; if you get cold, on goes the heater. We all do it to some degree but if you are good at it, life will surely be boring. What's wrong with contrast, pushing the boundaries, being a little scared, moving outside your comfort zone, getting a little hot or cold? Say 'yes' for a change. Life is meant to be about emotion with its ups and downs, highs and lows. If there are no extremes above and below the line, you will be very comfortable as a flat-liner, but life will be boring and you'll feel empty. Experiencing adrenalin, challenge, disappointment, joy, happiness, hot and cold is life itself. Sometimes it is meant to be raw.

I believe there is nothing as good as giving yourself to your partner. It makes life so real and sometimes nothing else matters. It is all you need when all else fails, especially when you are well below the line.

Sailing the world in my twenties, I discovered

myself and that you work to live, not live to work. If
you believe in only one thing, you must believe in
yourself. If you abuse yourself, how can you enjoy
a fulfilling life? No one is perfect, and we are all different, but surely the evidence is there: cigarettes
and alcohol are drugs, they are bad for your body and
soul, shortening your life. While some people die
living their dream on the side of a mountain, it is
not quite the same to say for a smoker, 'He died
doing what he loved best'! I believe good health is
a wonderful thing and, hey, you can't do much without it.

So here I am about to enter my fifties. I still gaze
at the stars, contemplating the big picture. The
meteor strike is now mainstream media with no
fixed date, and poor Random House, who have been
trying to get these few words out of me for nine
months. Over the past two I had had regular weekly
phone calls about deadlines, and each week I would
tell them 'tomorrow', only to be distracted by life.
There have been diving expeditions in Vanuatu, two
major car rallies, an ultralight float plane to bring
from Sydney to Tasmania, my 22-metre expedition
schooner *ICE* to truck cross-country from Darwin
to Yamba, three weeks in the French Riviera sorting
out a boat, property developments to coordinate,
this summer's Antarctic expedition to organise, and
helicopter lessons.

But today, no more deadline extensions! It's
finished! I am sending my essay by fax from the boat
as I head north to the Great Barrier Reef and Papua

New Guinea for three months of fishing, diving and exploring.

You are a long time dead, don't waste it!

Shaun Micallef

Shaun Micallef is a TV comedy writer and performer. His credits include *The Micallef Program*, *The Micallef Programme*, and *The Micallef Pogram*. His debits include *Welcher and Welcher*. Born in Adelaide in 1962 and abandoned shortly thereafter Shaun was raised by wolves and has only just learned to read and write. His heroin addiction, sex change operation, and affiliation with the Black Panther movement are behind him now and today he dedicates his life to building and designing leper colonies in Perth. Unfortunately, because leprosy is hard to come by in this country, most of the inhabitants of the Micallef Leper Estates in Alkimos suffer from lesser skin ailments like eczema and seborrheic dermatitis. Pity.

Volo Ergo Sum

People laugh when I tell them I was on the barricades in '68. It's probably the high squeaky voice I employ for such conversations – a fatal error if you wish to be taken seriously, and one of the myriad which litter my life as a political agitator, rebel thinker and Kerouakian ne'er-do-well. Few people realise I was on the barricades in '69 and '70 as well. It wasn't as crowded by then and so a lot easier to perch on. And the view! *Magnifique!* Still, try impressing a girl with *that* on the rue Geoffroy-Marie at three in the morning and she'll give you a stare cold enough to chill a cryogenics lab. Of course I should add that I am not arguing such obvious rodomotande should be used to pull the birds – there must be some sort of firm ideology behind it as well or they'll see through you quick smart.

Most people hammer out a vague code of ethics by the time they're thirty. With me it took longer. In fact I'm almost seventy now and I'm still working on it. But as I've gone a'promenading down the road less travelled over the years, my oar turning to a winnowing fan, I have jotted down some of my musings on life as they've occurred to me. True, my journals and notebooks taken together would fill the Queen Mary several times over (and not the boat either – I'm talking about the actual monarch), so I've tried to find a single entry which sort of sums up my philosophy of life, and cut it down a little so it'll fit into the 600 word limit for this squib – for which the chisellers at Random are not paying me a cent by the way – and which I am told I must adhere to on pain of being edited down by that butcher Marsden.

Anyhoo, here goes . . .

I was in Helsinki in 1948 buying some cufflinks when someone in our group suggested we pay a visit to Sibelius who lived nearby. We were all drunk so this seemed like a good idea, and we hailed a passing pony-and-trap and hightailed it into the verdant countryside of Hammenlinna three hours away. Unfortunately not only was Sibelius not at home, he had never lived there. According to the bald and startled man who answered the door no-one at all famous had even so much as set foot in his cottage in the sixty years he had been there (although he said something in fractured English about Noel Coward having popped in earlier that day and eating all his pound cake).

On the way back to Helsinki, however, the pony-and-trap driver told us a little parable which I thought worth recording. We stopped by the nearby Finnvox Studios and laid one down:

'There was an old man who lived atop a tall mountain for his whole life. His only contact with the outside world was to lower milk from his goats in a bucket on a rope to a small boy who lived in the valley, who would then sell the milk at the docks at the Port of Zeebrugge for six markka a tonne. The small boy would then dutifully return to the valley, put the day's takings in the bucket, and the old man would haul it up the mountain again – but not a word of thanks to the boy. He did this every day for ninety years. And when he died, you know what they found under his bed?'

We all shook our heads.

'Four furniture coasters. Yep – that old guy sure knew how to look after his carpet.'

From that day to this I have never been able to listen to Hjalmar Munsterhjelm's *Before the Thunderstorm* in quite the same way again. Mind you, it is a painting.

My message? The credo I live by? Don't worry

about face creams, plastic surgery, or looking slim. People get old, just face it. You want to be immortal, have some children . . .

Also, don't watch television current affairs programs or read women's magazines – they're crap.

WALTER MIKAC

Named one of Australia's 'national treasures', Walter Mikac is well known for his lobbying on gun control and helped to bring about much-needed reform. After losing his family in the Port Arthur shootings, he established The Alannah and Madeleine Foundation, a charity which assists child victims. Walter is remarried with a daughter.

Standing gnarled and crooked, the passage of decades was evident. If only the folds and wrinkles could speak. Bowed limbs stood testament to a life-time of nurturing.

My bonsai had outlived the blind old man who had generously given it to me. I hope he sensed by my silence how mesmerised I was. All the love and devotion he'd poured into this living thing was now mine to continue. Momentarily daunted by the proposition I wondered if my daughter might still be watering this tree well after my departure; a family heirloom. I fertilised and watered it with something akin to reverence. It would at times provoke thoughts of what happens after death. What would people remember most about me? Humour, crankiness, craziness, positivity, love, stubbornness, a healthy appetite for good food and wine?

It's a question many don't care to think about for

fear of confronting their own mortality. We like to think the story goes on forever! The answer to my lingering question was right there in front of me: the years of love that went into nurturing this tree. It's the years of love I best recall of the family I lost. Love. The deeds and thoughts that flow from it can conquer all. Headlines of bombings, terrorism, and violence barrage us to the point where we're becoming desensitised. Evil seems to be the prevailing theme. But this I truly believe: love can survive all and everything. It will ultimately triumph over the power of destruction and revenge.

Take a moment to look back on your favourite childhood memories. Mine gravitate around family outings. Going to Croatian picnics where family after family somehow seemed related to my parents and thereby me. More cousins than kids in my class, wow! Seeing the Sydney Harbour Bridge for the first time. Mum's constant outpourings of delight from the kitchen. Games of football, golf and squash with my dad and brothers. Dad trying to impress by letting us hit him in the guts, or careering into the squash wall in a vain attempt to win the vital point. The good and – more predominant – bad deeds of my youth. Saving for my first car and the agony of writing off my second. As I scroll back over my life, love is the overwhelming factor. It persists through failure, sadness and helplessness. It won't sink, be buried, hurried or brushed aside. People shouldn't underestimate the all-encompassing power of love.

Just like my bonsai needs water, nutrients and air, I surround myself with my wonderful wife, family and friends. The simple things. The things that mean most, but are sometimes not realised until they are gone. Sharing a joke, a song, cards, or reminiscing about times past. I believe that love is what makes this such a fantastic place to be. Each morning I tell myself how lucky I am. I love and am loved. And my prized bonsai sits in the corner to remind me, cared for now by my new daughter.

SHERYLE MOON

Sheryle Moon is renowned across Australia as a business leader, author and public speaker. A Director of Manpower Services Australia, Sheryle is also a Director on a number of public and private sector boards. She is the Strategic IT Advisor to CrimTrac. She is an Adjunct Professor at the University of Canberra, and an Honorary Ambassador for the ACT.

Sheryle is the author of *SelfScape – Success through Balance*, a practical guide to implementing personal success strategies. She also authored the *SET for Life* Report.

In 1999, she was named the Australian Business Woman of the Year. Sheryle is married with three children.

My father drank himself to death believing that opportunity had passed him by. I believe opportunity knocks more than once. I believe that the same opportunity is presented to individuals multiple times and that saying 'No' to the first knock does not mean you will be disadvantaged. Sometimes the first knock of opportunity can be the 'taste test' for what is around the corner. It gives you a glimpse of the new option so that you can adjust to the idea and next time grasp it with both hands.

There have been many occasions when the same opportunity has kept coming back to knock on my door. This has happened in my career and in love.

When I was in my early thirties, a momentous love affair ended quite badly. My heart was truly broken and the ensuing few months were the worst time I had ever known. I was only beginning to face a life without the man I thought was my soul mate. One morning, I was sitting in a cafe in Paddington in Sydney. Over my cappuccino rim I spied two tangled lovers at another table. In tears, I sat rigid, feeling guilty for watching such an intimate moment and unbearably desolate. The waitress came to deliver my toast and as she put it on the table she said; 'Your heart will heal. A window has been opened for you to see what love can be. Next time you will understand the importance of the relationship.'

I scoffed and started to cry again. Two months later I was sent on a training course in place of a sick colleague. There I met the man with whom I have now shared twenty years of my life. He and my previous lover have unusual names, were born in the same month of the same year and have joie de vivre in everything they do.

In 1998 I received a letter from the convenor of the Telstra Australian Business Women of the Year Awards saying I had been nominated for the title. My nominator was an executive in a client company. To enter required a lengthy application process and at the time I was just about to travel overseas on a work-related assignment. I also felt that I did not fit my idea of what the winner of such an award would have achieved. Had I really made a difference with

Sheryle Moon

my work? Had I contributed above and beyond hundreds of other women in my life? In my view I had not! I wrote to Telstra telling them how I felt and declining the opportunity to proceed.

Twelve months later, I received another letter from Telstra telling me I had been nominated for the awards. Again I was nominated by an executive in a client company. Opportunity was clearly knocking again, but was I ready, or deserving of the title? I pondered long and hard before I decided to open the door and let opportunity in. I wrote the application with help from many work colleagues. They were part of my success in winning the award in 1999 just as they were part of my success each and every day.

When opportunity knocks but you are not ready, do not despair. Recognise that this is the first knock. Opportunity will wait and return to your door. Then it will start ringing the bell as well as knocking and you will know that the time is now right for you to embrace this opportunity with passion and commitment. I believe this.

217

PETER MOORE

Peter Moore is an author from Sydney who has been described as 'The Australian Bill Bryson'. His books include *The Wrong Way Home*, which saw him travelling overland from London to Sydney, *Swahili for the Broken-Hearted*, an account of a journey from Cape Town to Cairo, and *Vroom with a View*, where he went in search of Italy's *dolce vita* on a 1961 Vespa. At last count he had visited 93 countries and written six books. When he is not travelling he can be found in either Sydney or London watching his collection of Skippy DVDs.

SKIPPY THE BUSH KANGAROO IS THE BEST GOODWILL AMBASSADOR AUSTRALIA HAS EVER HAD

Over the years my travels have taken me to some pretty off-beat corners of the world. Albania. The Sudan. The suburbs of Brisbane. But no matter how far-flung these places are, there always seems to be one particular Australian who has been there before me. Skippy. As in Skippy the Bush Kangaroo.

It's hardly surprising. Between 1968 and 1971 ninety-one episodes of Skippy were made and exported to over eighty countries. So wherever I slap my Aussie passport down, chances are the immigration officer on duty has seen the show and will greet me with a little kangaroo impression – tucking their elbows up under their armpits and doing a fair approximation of Skip's legendary '*tsking*'. Experience has taught me that a smile and a quick kangaroo impersonation back is the best and quickest way to get my passport stamped. It's quite a surreal experience – especially in Afghanistan where there were hair-triggered mujahideen wandering around with AK-47s just outside the door.

I think it's quite endearing that we are best known as a country full of furry animals that can open gates and play the piano. Sure, our intelligentsia would prefer that we were known for our art, literature and advances in science. And it rankles that Americans still think there are kangaroos bouncing down our main streets. But if these misconceptions bring a smile to people's faces when they think of Australia, I reckon that's a good thing.

I've certainly benefited from the goodwill Skip has spread around the world. In Tehran a taxi driver invited me back to his family's apartment on the strength of the show. I got to sit on the couch with him and his young son, sipping lemonade freshly made by his wife, and watch a taped episode of Skippy that had been dubbed into Farsi. The rough tones of an Ayatollah quite suited Ranger Matt Hammond.

'We like Skippy,' the taxi driver explained, bouncing his son on his knee. 'No sex, no drugs.' In this part of Tehran at least, Australia was perceived as a place with values that resonated throughout the world, not part of a coalition busy imposing America's will on the world.

In Gabon it was Skip's roughhouse abilities that came to my rescue. I inadvertently walked into the meanest bar in a mining town in the jungle in the east of the country just as a bunch of ill-tempered miners came off their shift. They eyed me with great suspicion until an episode of Skippy came on. Our favourite Eastern Grey kicked open a door, pulled antivenom from her pouch and disarmed gun-wielding villains. Not only was I given more respect after the show – they weren't sure now what I'd pull out of my backpack if cornered – but I didn't have to buy a drink for the rest of the afternoon.

The most telling example of Skippy's power for good, however, came when I was in Ethiopia researching *Swahili for the Broken-Hearted*. I got caught in the middle of riots in Addis Ababa, sheltering in a coffin shop while an angry mob overturned and set fire to cars just outside. When the worst had passed I emerged onto the street only to be confronted by the looters pointing at me and yelling 'American! American!' A young Ethiopian stepped in and spoke to them in Amharic and I was allowed to pass unharmed.

'I told them you were Australian,' he explained. 'They have seen your Skippy.'

Somehow I don't think a working knowledge of John Howard and his policies would have had quite the same effect.

DI MORRISSEY

Di Morrissey is Australia's most popular female author.

Is there ever a time when one can pause and say, I am happy, I have done well, I am content?

In striving to get to these desirable states, it seems to me we run past them in our haste and don't notice we are, at some particular moment, happy, achieving and content. We hurry to the destination without enjoying the journey.

In these times of international upheaval and conflict, where greed is ruining our planet, where corruption flourishes and the abandoned and fleeing are ignored, where the elderly are disregarded, when youth sees only limited possibilities and few aspire to follow . . . it is sometimes difficult to see a rainbow of hope and happy tomorrows.

But I am sunny by nature (or genes or happenstance), a positive person who refuses to give up, give in, and I face each morning with a smile. If I don't believe that we can, and must, do something about the dark clouds hovering, about making life better for all, then I believe I would not be here. So I *do* believe . . .

I believe . . .

. . . We can grasp at dreams. Be who we want no

matter what anyone else tells us. We can choose a path that makes us fulfilled individuals. That it is all right to nurture oneself and pursue ambitions for intrinsically personal reasons.

. . . That abundant material possessions, money, and acknowledgement by others is not going to make me a happier or better person. We can make an effort to help others – and that includes our family and outsiders – which teaches us how valuable we can be. I believe we can learn to like ourselves, and know that it is all right to fail, or disagree, or take a risk, or follow our instinct.

. . . It is essential we talk about our fears, our dreams, our needs. That in sharing, without demands or dependence, we can come to a closer understanding of how to listen to the other. We can make changes in our life. We can be alone; for moments or months, and treasure this as a time of peace, reflection, learning and growth.

. . . We are all equal in this world. We may not have equal possessions, opportunities, help or hope but we can make this possible.

. . . In the goodness of humankind, despite what we see around us. I believe we all have an obligation to make things more equal. A fairer distribution of wealth, food, power and happiness in daily life. That we must speak out when we see unjustness and corruption. Listen to the muffled cries of the oppressed and less fortunate. Heed our own sense of compassion and act upon it. For in doing, not criticising or complaining, we engage in bringing change. Small determined steps, where we avoid the potholes and speedsters, will carry us more surely on our journey rather than will a blind charge.

. . . We can empower ourselves to be and to do better. We can make time in our lives for small kind gestures, periods of contemplation, and appreciation of others.

. . . If we look into our hearts, our mindset, our beliefs and actions and know we have to be account-able . . . somewhere, sometime . . . then I believe we can live our lives as they were meant to be. It is up to us to remember this commitment – that each of us can contribute to a significantly happier world – by believing we can.

JOANNA MURRAY-SMITH

Joanna Murray-Smith is a Melbourne playwright and novelist. Her novels include *Judgement Rock* (2002) and *Truce* (1994), both published by Penguin. Her plays have been performed throughout Australia and around the world. They include *Rapture*, *Nightfall*, *Redemption*, *Love-Child*, *Bombshells* and *Honour*, which was produced on Broadway and recently at The National Theatre in London. Her work has been nominated for many awards and both *Honour* and *Rapture* won Victorian Premier's Literary Awards for Drama.

Ingmar Bergman once said that some things 'should be allowed to exist in a half light'. The older I become, the greater truth I see in this. For so many of our early years, we strive to know, to understand, to clarify things. More recently I have realised, that in terms of love and art and nature, mystery can not only be useful, but more dependable. We construct answers because we're frightened of not knowing, but coming to accept the shadows is the pleasurable part of growing older. It is within the unknown that the imagination flourishes, unstopped by fact or certainty. It is also in the shadows that love and all its associated experiences are expressed, since the human capacity to feel is so extravagant and contradictory. Great art, as well as ordinary wisdom, comes from letting the shadows alone, from expressing or inhabiting them, without trying to illuminate them.

Allowing the strangeness of feelings to exist without always determining motives and explanations is a very delicate process of release. I have learned it, a little, through having children. Once I believed that parents owned their children, they mastered them and possessed them. I believed this, even having been a child. Now I know that children teach adults things they cannot learn through any other means: about faith, fear and humility. Children find their own way, experience things distinctly from their creators, feel love in different ways and ultimately triumph through their separateness. It's hard to accept as a parent, because to begin with it feels to be a diminishing, but ultimately it is a witnessing of tremendous beauty and a mutual freeing.

I spend most of my life trying to balance a yearning for peace and a yearning for agitation. Writing feeds both these impulses simultaneously. I think that this is a fundamental quandary for most people. We long for safety and we also long for adventure. Perhaps child-having, like writing, satisfies both appetites, since children are so terrifying, but not usually life-threatening! They are the ultimate antidote to boredom, because they defy order and certainty. In their small faces are all the great mysteries: mortality, love, ambivalence. They make fear manifold, but also happiness. This, too, is central to

Bergman's shadows. Our feelings are bigger and stronger than our intellects, they encompass opposites all at once, they defy ideology and elegance, but they make life interesting.

FRANCESCA NAISH

Naturopath and author Francesca Naish was born, educated and grew up in England, coming to Australia in her late twenties after varied careers in computers, theatre (stage and street), circus, health food and other pursuits. In Australia she combined her interests in natural health and women's issues, and commenced a career as a naturopath, specialising in natural fertility management and reproductive health, and pioneering the concept and practice of preconception health care for prospective parents.

She is the founder and director of the Jocelyn Centre, Australia's first naturopathic clinic devoted to helping women and couples manage their fertility effectively and conceive healthy, happy babies, and of Natural Fertility Management Pty Ltd, through which she trains health professionals in Australia and overseas in her methods. She is the author of *The Lunar Cycle* and *Natural Fertility*, and the co-author (with Janette Roberts) of *The Natural Way to Better Babies*, *The Natural Way to Better Pregnancy*, *The Natural Way to Better Birth and Bonding*, and *The Natural Way to Better Breastfeeding*. Many of these titles have been published internationally. She appears frequently in the media, and is a popular speaker and lecturer.

Belief is a funny thing. Believing things often makes us feel better – but we have to be sure we don't

227

believe them *just because* they make us feel better.

Or, if we take as given that human happiness is synonymous with the greatest good, we could believe that things are good *because* they make us feel better, though perhaps we need to be sure that they don't make someone else feel worse.

For example:

Laughing makes me feel better, so I believe that laughing is good.

Loving makes me feel better, so I believe that loving is good.

Doing things well makes me feel better, so I believe that this is also good.

Of course, we can also apply this to others. When something I do makes others feel better, I feel better too – and I believe that this is good.

Luckily, laughing, loving and achieving usually make everyone feel better, so it's a win–win situation (and who wouldn't believe in that?).

Of course some people, and all people some of the time, feel better when they make others feel bad, because it gives them power. Power can feel very good, and this can be exciting, but it's also dangerous. I try to be mindful of this.

Others believe that they can hand over ultimate responsibility to another more powerful being. For some people this may be God, or a higher secular or familial authority. This makes them feel good. It doesn't make me feel good – I believe that this is a cop-out.

So I suppose, deep down, I believe that we are responsible for the good or the bad that we do, and that it's up to us to do our best, and make a difference to the world where we can.

Everyone's best is different, but when we do our best, we feel good. And, even better, we probably make a difference to the sum of good feeling in the world, and help to spread it around.

However, I also believe that it's deeply important to have compassion for those who find it hard to be their best, and that includes ourselves. Forgiving ourselves for our own shortcomings is essential if we want to move on.

If, at the end of my life, I can say I did my best (at least most of the time) and I made a difference (however small) to the balance of happiness and suffering in the world, then I believe that this is probably as good as it gets.

Along the way I believe it's absolutely important to laugh a lot; to love a lot; to give my full energy and commitment to the tasks that fall in my path; to speak out when I see injustice, destruction and suffering; to embrace the disappointments, despair, pain and struggles that are part of any full life, but to reject cruelty, intolerance and greed; to live a healthy life; to tread gently on the earth, and to do the least harm that I can.

Also, I believe that every time I compromise these beliefs, I harm myself and others, and weigh the balance on the down side.

So how do I, you, or any of us, contribute to the well-being of the world? And is this a relevant question?

I believe it to be important to have respect for all life – human, animal and plant – and to care for our environment, our minds, our bodies, and those of our children.

I devoted the first part of my adult life to exploring the boundaries of consciousness and behaviour, and the difference between accepted reality and the world of imagination and ideas. This was a lot of fun, but left me with more questions than answers.

The second part of my life has been more pragmatic, trying to provide some answers, dedicated to my children and my work with natural and holistic health, and acting on my belief that nature and nurture can combine to support healthy minds and bodies, through responsible ecological lifestyles.

But, ultimately, I can only say that this is true for me, and that for every answer there is always another question. I have to live by my beliefs, however imperfectly, and my core belief is that it is of ultimate importance to do so. However, I also believe that we can get 'stuck' in our belief systems and that they can be limiting, and that questions can be more valuable than answers, because they lead you onwards.

ALASTAIR NICHOLSON

The Honourable Alastair Bothwick Nicholson, AO, RFD, was born on 19 August 1938 and educated at Scotch College and Melbourne University. He was appointed a Justice of the Supreme Court of Victoria in 1982, Chief Justice of the Family Court of Australia in 1988, and a Justice of the Federal Court of Australia in 1988. He retired as a Justice of the Federal Court of Australia on 31 May 2004, and as Chief Justice of the Family Court of Australia on 3 July 2004. He received the appointment as an Officer of the Order of Australia in 1992 and is a former President of the International Association of Family and Conciliation Courts. He and his wife, Mrs Nicholson, were for many years members of Kids in Care, a group providing emergency foster care to children and on many occasions they acted as foster parents for such children. Since 1984 he has been the Chairman of the ACSO Centre which is a charitable organisation devoted to the provision of care, accommodation and counselling to ex-prisoners of both sexes. He is a patron of the Child and Family Care Network, the Melbourne Wildlife Sanctuary and the Hawthorn Fooftball Club. He is also a member of the Advisory Board of the Alannah and Madeline Foundation and chairs a Coalition against Bullying supported by that organisation. On 1 April 2004 he was bestowed with the title of Professor AB Nicholson AO, RFD, Honorary Professorial Fellow, Criminology Department, University of Melbourne.

He has three daughters, his first grandson born in August 2000 and his second in February 2002.

In order to identify one's beliefs, it is necessary to examine their source.

For most of us the obvious source starts with our parents. In my case their influence was overwhelmingly positive. My parents, like myself, were not churchgoers; indeed for most of their married life they lived far from any church, but they had been brought up in families with positive Christian values. I stress the word positive, because there are also negative values associated with Christianity. The positive ones as I see them are consideration for the feelings of one's fellows, a sense of duty towards those less fortunate, a belief in the equality of human beings, a belief in justice and fairness coupled with mercy and the rejection of dishonourable behaviour in all its forms.

An early experience was exposure to the racist attitudes that typified Australia's administration of post war Papua–New Guinea. It was an unconscious racism that still permeates Australian culture and partly explains our attitude to Indigenous people. As a young person I accepted it and it was only later, with greater maturity, that I realised how wrong it was.

Another source of beliefs stems from the educative process. I attended a church school as a boarder for nine years prior to going to University. I doubt that the school's religious teaching had much influence upon me, except in a negative sense. However the former students of the school had a long and honourable history of service to their country. The ethos of the school recognised the importance of this and recognised the duty that lies with the educational opportunity that it offered. I accepted this as an important value and one that I have tried to act upon.

Another effect that the school had upon me was a recognition that it is important to stand by your beliefs and to speak out against injustices. There was in a sense an unintended consequence, in that I rebelled against the conformist nature of the society that the school represented. Most students came from well off conservative families and the ethos of the school tended to equate political conservatism with proper behaviour, which was an approach that I rejected, sometimes to my own cost both then and since.

The much freer attitudes engendered by residence at a university college also helped me appreciate the need for tolerance and freedom of thought and speech.

Another major factor that has influenced my beliefs has been the history of the 19th and 20th Centuries and in particular the suffering that was brought about in those centuries by war, tyrannical regimes and religious persecution. Particular features of the worst of these regimes were the destruction of the rule of law and the compliant politicians, judges and bureaucrats who helped to bring this about. This has strengthened my belief that it is the duty of all of us to speak out against this sort of behaviour. Tyrants are encouraged by silence.

These attitudes are not only to be found in dictatorships, but also in democracies, as I believe that recent events have exemplified. In an Australian context I have in mind the treatment of asylum seekers and their children, the involvement of this country in the war in Iraq, the neglect of the rights of persons under a disability and particularly of children, and our continued failure to discharge our responsibilities to Indigenous people.

If there is one beacon of light in this darkness it is the human rights movement that arose as a result of the horrors of the 19th and 20th Centuries. This commenced with organisations like Red Cross and the early Geneva Conventions and extended to the formation of the League of Nations and later the United Nations. In turn this led to the foundation of organisations like UNICEF and international acceptance of such instruments as the International Covenant on Civil and Political Rights, The Convention for the Elimination of All Forms of Discrimination against Women and the United Nations Convention on the Rights of the Child and many others.

It is currently fashionable for conservatives to decry the United Nations and the validity of such instruments. This is a barren doctrine. In my view they represent the only way forward. They transcend religious and national boundaries and provide a code of conduct that has the potential to do much to eliminate the world's problems. If these principles are set aside, one has to ask the question 'What is left?'

It is obviously no answer to refer to religious or moral principles, since these differ from religion to religion or ideology to ideology. Outside these international instruments there is no universally accepted set of guidelines for controlling national and international behaviour. They provide what I believe to be a genuine source of hope and aspiration for all of us. It is no answer to point to instances of non observance, or even that our own country sometimes acts in flagrant breach of them, provided that such breaches are recognised for what they are and exposed to public gaze and criticism. In the absence of a guiding set of principles we are left with such gloomy concepts as might is right and the end justifies the means.

ERIC NEAL

Sir Eric Neal, AC, CVO, has enjoyed a varied and successful career from its beginnings as a trade apprentice, to professional engineer, corporate executive, Chief Commissioner of the Sydney City Council, director of a number of well known Australian companies, to State Governor of South Australia and currently Chancellor of the Flinders University of South Australia.

He has lived in Adelaide, Broken Hill, Ballarat, Brisbane and Sydney and served on corporate boards in Niugini, the Pacific Islands, Indonesia, Malaysia, the USA and UK. He has served as Chair of the Duke of Edinburgh's Award Program in Australia, of Opera Foundation Australia, and the organising committee of the 1986 Commonwealth Study Conference.

The foundations of my personal philosophy were laid in my childhood which incidentally was a very happy one, despite it being during the time of the Great Depression of the 1930s. Unemployment levels were around 24 per cent and there were no unemployment cash benefits, but food chits were available. Those who were in full employment, and my father was one of these, did what they could to help the unemployed, an example of good citizenship which has remained with me.

I was raised as the eldest of four children by loving parents who taught me basic Christian values, values that to me are unchanging in a world that is continually undergoing change.

Those values included the need to work hard and study, to be honest, not to lie or cheat, to treat people as you want to be treated, to be 'slow to chide and swift to bless', and to be loyal.

They also taught me that while the Christian faith and its values were important, what was less important was the venue, and the means, by which that faith was conveyed or transmitted.

Our family was Anglican, but as young children we attended the local Methodist Church and Sunday School because it was closer to home; as we grew older we walked the longer distance to the Anglican Church where I was ultimately confirmed.

My wife-to-be was a regular church-attender, also an Anglican. Her sense of values is similar to my own, which has helped in the making of a long and happy marriage. She has instilled those values into our two sons, of whom we are very proud.

During a long and reasonably successful business career, which led to the position of Managing Director of a company employing 25,000 people, I endeavoured to follow those same values that I had grown up with in my dealings with staff, customers, suppliers and unions. The standards set by the top management of any organisation ultimately become the standards of the whole organisation.

Aside from legal commitments, one's word should

become one's bond, and one should never make a commitment one is not prepared to keep. If one is seeking a happy and fulfilling life, material possessions are less important than one's good name. Obviously it is an advantage if one is able to enjoy both!

An important observation that came to me during my visits to a great number of countries of the world is that the great religious faiths of the world are based upon a set of values, or code of conduct, for people to live by, in peace and harmony with their fellow man. We should respect the beliefs of people of other faiths; the important thing, in my view, is for people to have a set of values and a code of conduct to live by.

My wife and I have enjoyed a happy and rewarding life. This has not been the case with many others less fortunate than us, but we both believe that one of the responsibilities that we all have as community members is to do what we can to help those who, through no fault of their own, are facing hardship, poverty or ill-health. Through our married life we have enjoyed devoting time to worthy community causes. I am continually impressed by the huge numbers of volunteers in our community who devote their time, skills and energy to helping those less fortunate than themselves. It reinforces one's faith in people.

GUSTAV NOSSAL

Sir Gustav Nossal, AC, CBE, FAA, FRS, was born in Austria in 1931 and came to Australia with his family in 1939. He studied Medicine at the University of Sydney and took his PhD at the Walter and Eliza Hall Institute of Medical Research in Melbourne. Apart from two years as Assistant Professor of Genetics at Stamford University, one year at the Pasteur Institute in Paris, and one year as Special Consultant to the World Health Organisation, Nossal's entire research career has been at the Hall Institute, which he served as Director (1965–1996). Nossal was also Professor of Medical Biology at the University of Melbourne.

Nossal's research is in fundamental immunology, and he has written five books and 530 scientific articles in this and related fields. He has been President of the International Union of Immunological Societies (1986–89); President of the Australian Academy of Science (1994–98); a member of the Prime Minister's Science, Engineering and Innovation Council (1987–96); Chairman of the committee overseeing the World Health Organisation's Vaccines and Biologicals Program (1993–2002); and Chairman of the Strategic Advisory Council of the Bill and Melinda Gates Children's Vaccine Program (1998–2003).

Nossal was knighted in 1977, made a Companion of the Order of Australia in 1989 and appointed Australian of the Year in 2000. He has received numerous other prestigious

honours from eleven countries. Nossal is also involved in
charitable work as Chairman of the Felton Bequests' Committee; in the business community as a Principal of Foursight
Associates Pty Ltd; and in the international advancement
of Australia as Chairman of the Global Foundation Advisory
Council. He was also involved in Aboriginal affairs as Deputy
Chairman of the Council for Aboriginal Reconciliation (1998–
2000).

Are science and spirituality in conflict? No, they are
not antagonistic but rather complementary ways of
seeing and learning. The essence of science is the
systematic accumulation of objective and verifiable
knowledge about the material world and universe.
This is a powerful way of satisfying the curiosity
within all of us. At the same time, there exists in
every person a longing for transcendence, a thirst
for value and meaning in life, a search for answers to
questions which science cannot address. Why am I
here? Where am I going? What is life all about? These
metaphysical questions are approached through the
humanities, philosophy, theology and religion, of
course, but also history, art, literature and sociology.
One can learn a lot about the phenomenon of man
by studying Charles Darwin, or the genetic revolu-
tion ushered in by James Watson or Francis Crick.
Equally human nature is revealed by reading Homer
or William Shakespeare. From the great religions,
which all share core values, we can learn much about
how individuals might strive for inner growth and
perfection, and how they should interact with one

another to build better societies.

I believe firmly in evolution by natural selection, but note that nature in its raw state is pretty cruel. The survival of the fittest is often at the cost of the less fit. Buried in our selfish DNA there is a dark side of human nature which can be cruel and warlike, intolerant and racist, and this dark side is frequently not far below the surface. Counterbalancing this are civilisation and education, promoting the kinder, gentler side which encourages unselfish behaviour, seeks harmony with others and prompts reflection and deeper self knowledge. I believe one of the main purposes of life is to learn to cultivate this latter side and control the former.

Science is making great strides in fields like neuro-physiology and brain chemistry and has powerful things to say about the biochemical processes under-lying deep emotions. Once again, these cannot supplant the insights we obtain to our joy in the beauty of nature, the peace which comes from being in harmony with those surrounding us, the dizzy ecstasy of maternal love, from our own experiences and via the humanities. Spirituality and science can co-exist comfortably. Nevertheless, some extreme positions taken in the name of religion do offend me greatly. Top of the list is creationism. The literal interpretation of the Book of Genesis, where the world was created in just six days, with all the species ready-made, and all just four thousand years ago, flies in the face of overwhelming evidence. It mocks biology and geology to an equal degree. This is one of many examples where we need to decide what, in the great faiths, is to be taken literally, and what represents a powerful and beautiful metaphor.

I believe we must all struggle mightily to reduce the huge gap in living standards, educational possibilities and health outcomes between industrialised and developing countries. Equally we must address the gaps between rich and poor right here in Australia. This is most urgent with respect to our Aboriginal and Torres Strait Islander populations. We can make progress if we have the will and the generosity.

RACHAEL OAKES-ASH

Rachael Oakes-Ash never shies away from a confronting issue. She spoke her first word at eight months, and ate her first solids a month later and has been speaking between mouthfuls ever since. The author of the candid autobiography *Good Girls Do Swallow* and the controversial *Anything She Can Do I Can Do Better* about female competition, Rachael is a renowned social commentator. She works as a radio announcer, television presenter, documentary producer and corporate speaker and has won numerous awards including the Women's Electoral Lobby Edna Ryan Award for Humour, for using wit to promote women's interests.

My father is a wise man, though I did not know it when I was young. He warned me about my friends he thought would let me down, he told me persistence, hard work and belief would get me ahead in life and that success is about daring. Of course I didn't listen, preferring to forge ahead with my own life and friends, only to realise later that what I have learned is what he tried to teach me all along.

Life is like that. It's cyclical. As I grow older I hear my mother's voice escape my lips with words I swore I would never repeat. That's the nature of the mother–daughter relationship. By the time you realise what a brave woman she is, you're a woman yourself.

When it comes to life beliefs, it takes life to form them. When I was five years old I believed I was immortal, now at thirty-six with arthritis I know I am not. At seventeen years of age I thought I was the best driver on the road; a number of accidents, scrapes and bumps later I believe everyone else thinks they are. At twenty-five years of age I believed the world owed me; ten years later I believe I now owe the world.

I could list the beliefs I have inherited in my life but they would not be mine to list. So I shall list what I have observed and learned, with the knowledge that those beliefs may change yet again:

Stretch marks are the road maps of where we have been in our life and cellulite is the hail damage we receive along the way.

Human cloning has already happened. Just visit a shopping mall during high school holidays and see if you can distinguish Natalie from Nicole.

If diets worked we would only ever need to diet once in our lives to achieve our goal weight, but try telling this to Jenny Craig's bank manager.

There will always be people who don't like you and always people who do, so why dance around the ones that don't, shouting 'Pick me, pick me!'? If you strive to be liked by everyone you will always be disliked by one – yourself.

Always compare and you will always despair.

We can have it all, just not all at once.

A woman's womb and marital status is not public property and not open for public comment.

There is nothing quiet about the silent treatment.

Some friendships have use-by dates and others a life-time guarantee.

There is no community in a global village.

Business management is about people not paper, no matter how many management reports are written.

You won't know unless you ask.

To be different invites ridicule and exclusion from the mediocre.

Inspiration and energy are contagious, but wealth isn't.

Without a deadline the work never gets done. With a deadline it will be done the night before.

Own who you are; speak up through your fear; your difference is what makes you unique. You are OK as you are and your flaws, not your perfections, are what make you interesting.

To be courageous is to be alive.

Wisdom comes with age. It's a cliché but like most clichés (including this one) it's true. As my parents grow older I understand them so much more and see them as human beings with their own fears, vulnerabilities and courage. While my belief system originally mirrored theirs until I defined myself, there is one belief my father told me that remains true: Believe in yourself and you can do anything.

Margaret Olley

Margaret Olley is regarded as Australia's most important 20th Century interior and still-life painter. With a career spanning more than fifty years, Olley's ability to capture the beauty and harmony in familiar, everyday objects has given her a place among Australia's finest artists.

Olley was born in 1923 in Lismore, New South Wales, and in 1945 received first class honours in the Arts Diploma course at East Sydney Technical College. She held her first solo exhibition in 1948, which was a great success – both the Art Gallery of New South Wales and the National Gallery of Victoria purchased paintings, as did influential private collectors.

In 1949 Olley made her first of several visits to Europe – to see and study the great art collections in London and Paris, as well as Spain, Portugal and Italy. Over her long and successful career Margaret has exhibited her work extensively and to great acclaim, and throughout her life continued to travel, visiting Papua New Guinea, Malaysia, Cambodia, Bali, America, Greece, China, Russia and Europe. She has won many prestigious prizes for art work and in 1991 she was awarded an honorary Doctorate of Letters by Macquarie University and was appointed Officer of the Order of Australia (AO).

Although Olley is inherently an Australian artist, her work is international and reflects her extensive travels and understanding of worldwide artistic trends and traditions. Her paintings reveal the breadth of internationalism that set her work apart from any mainstream art theory, or period.

THE COLOUR GREEN

I believe in the colour green. When this life-giving colour disappears from earth so do we. Green brings back memories of my early childhood in Tully, North Queensland. Tully has the highest rainfall in Australia. I can still hear the roar of rain, teeming down the broad-leafed foliages of Mount Tyson and smell the north's pungent odour of mingled growth and decay. We moved to a farm on the banks of the Tweed River in northern NSW and I breathed in a different smell, the sweet smell arising from the earth after rain had fallen on grass. It meant growth. I still wait for that sweetness. But now after rain, all I smell is tar.

I was brought up by kind and loving parents. Strong foundations of caring and giving were learnt at an early age. The kitchen was always the favourite place in the house. We watched my mother cooking, bottling fruit from the trees, making jams and cakes. There were eggs in abundance. Butter had to be churned, everyone took turns. We all sat down together for meals and grace was said to remind us to be grateful for what we received.

People were constantly coming to stay for holidays and my parents seemed to be always helping someone. My father had a huge vegetable garden beside the house. Watching everything grow was a source of such fascination and wonder to us children. We were encouraged to have our own plot, and to pick the beans and peas. It was the days of the Depression; we grew more than we needed and what we couldn't use was given away. The same happened with fish we caught.

Watching gardens grow and plants go through their cycle of life, over the years I've come to believe the solutions to problems can often be found in nature and the garden. Plants and people are really very similar. As the earth restores the life-giving colour of green to the garden after rain so should we be caring of each other and of our planet.

I have been given so much help and encouragement during my life that I believe strongly, following the example set by my parents, in giving back. Instead of sending probes – that take over six months to reach their destination, if they do – to search for water and signs of life on Mars, I wish some of the money could be spent on giving water to people on this Earth who are without it.

Mars, from photos sent back, looks very bleak, rather like what we have created here through centuries of mismanagement of natural resources. For example, we non-Indigenous people have only been in Australia for two hundred years and already our waterways are in a deplorable state. Cotton and rice crops that require so much water are grown in impossible places. Why not give the poor farmers the gift of growing hemp? This hardy plant was cultivated in ancient times in the cradle of civilisation Mesopotamia. It was used in the sails, rigging, sailors' uniforms and even the flags of the ships that bought us to Australia in the first place. Hemp needs little water, no insecticides and can have multiple usages including paper-making, which would stop wood-chipping. New employment opportunities would also be created.

If we could only learn to love and care for this fragile planet Earth, if we could clean up our clogged, endangered waterways and regrow forests, then the fast disappearing green may be replaced. If we do this, if we cherish the colour green, life will go on.

JAMES PENGELLEY

James Pengelley was born in 1986 in Perth, Western Australia. Graced with a notable visual impairment and more chest hair than permissible by Australian legislation, his aspiration to be a pilot fell through at the age of four and so, having recently completed his high school studies, his plans remain to study briefly at university before moving into the great void of social hierarchies and achieving personal satisfaction in whatever shape or form it decides to present itself.

His uncanny passion for sport, cooking, creative writing and other people's smiles has resulted in a strangely intriguing and charismatic creation – yet he remains confident that he is still fit for public consumption, if under suitable female supervision.

I know that I am slowly gathering dust like everyone else, and with each layer I acquire a new set of principles that sound humane and respectable and I call these my beliefs. In all honesty, I could probably write one hundred essays on what I believe in right now, and a hundred more essays on what I believed in yesterday.

Yet strangely enough, my issue is not deciding what I believe in, rather, choosing to write about something that will not become outdated faster than a new computer.

Now I feel myself sitting here, awe-inspired and 300 percent sure that I know what I want to say – but feeling hopelessly like a three-year-old with a vivid imagination, blowing up enemy trenches and shooting down spacecraft from the remnants of a backyard sandpit, for lack of my certainty of how to go about communicating the timeless, perennial features of my belief system.

The one entity that remains constant and forms the core of my great collection of beliefs, past and present, is me. I am my own heart and soul. I am the only person who believes what I believe. I am the only person who loves who and what I am capable of loving – I am the only one who loves loving all that I love.

I guess what I am suggesting is that at the heart of every radical adolescent idea that seeps through my skin, and every bad-taste fashion sense I choose to adopt, is the goodwill and pride on which I choose to found my life. And while my interests, obsessions, moods and appearance fluctuate, the only constant thing about me is the fact that I exist.

So this is what I choose to believe in. Me. I will always be around to facilitate, support and nourish whatever I choose to believe. If I were, for whatever reason, to reject myself and all that on which I choose to found my life, then I would become a walking contradiction.

I believe that I am the most important person in my life – however, acknowledging this means that I am capable of sharing my energy and focus with others. I do not believe that it is wrong to put your-self before others in most situations – if you do so as a statement of your belief in who you want to be.

From every new belief comes a better understand-ing of ourselves, along with that wave of emotion which scolds us for not better understanding our own existence but at the same time satisfies even the most insatiable emotional frustration.

I know who I am. I feel who I am. I believe who I am and I am adamant that learning to understand and accept ourselves is a journey everybody needs to make before they concern themselves with greater things.

MARGARET POMERANZ

Margaret Pomeranz began her career in film and television as a screenwriter during the 1970s. She joined SBS in 1980 and worked as writer/producer before launching *The Movie Show* with David Stratton in 1986. She recently began working with the ABC on *At the Movies*.

She is active on issues of free speech and public broadcasting. She is past President of the Film Critics Circle of Australia and is currently President of Watch on Censorship.

She is the mother of two adult children.

One weekend at our fibro shack on the coast after a noisy, laughter-filled lunch with friends and our now-adult kids, we all went for a walk along the beach. It was a beautiful sunny day, the group straggled along, forming and reforming into small pockets of conversation. I was pierced by a feeling of intense happiness. It was an awareness of joy.

I turned to my friend and said 'This is such a "bright shiny day"', and word passed around and we tried to sing the song and then we tried to remember who'd sung it.

It was silly. It was real.

What was it? Good food and wine, a sense of family, a sense of the sort of relaxed closeness you can only achieve with intimate friends. Being happy that your children have grown up to be nice, kind people. Being delighted that they can make you laugh hysterically. Being content that they seem to like you too.

I think love is underrated in the world. In defending free speech I've read a lot about what causes kids to go wrong. It can't be the movies or we'd have a much bigger problem on our hands. No, I think kids need to know they're loved. And with the pressure on families these days there's not a lot of space left, after exhaustion sets in, to create moments that are special.

I like Mark Latham's idea of reading to kids. I did. I most probably wouldn't have read *The Hobbit* without them, or come into contact with Roald Dahl's wonderfully seditious literature. It was more fun for me as they got older, that's for sure. Oh, and I think the kids got something out of it too.

If children can grow up to be confident about themselves, confident that the persons who know them best like and love them, then they are less likely to be suspicious about others, less likely to be scared of 'the other', less likely to cause harm in this world. They are going to feel valued.

I also believe in romantic love and pain and the whole damned thing. When you are in love you know you are accessing one of the secrets of the universe. And I don't believe love shrivels up and dies, not for me anyway. All the people I've truly loved are tucked up inside me, with their wisdoms remembered, the good times remembered, the bad times tossed away.

And going global, I'm still trying to believe that humankind is worth loving. What amazing act of evolution created us, with our ability to create the technical world we live in, to develop language and abstract thought, to create art and music and literature? How can we be stuffing it up so completely?

But love is an abstract. Being a practical person, the other quality I believe in is effort. One of the most significant others in my life said that loving is doing. Love without effort is just another four letter word.

Love is cooking. It's the effort of shopping, unpacking, peeling, dicing, searing, serving. It's something you do for people you love.

Love is taking your ten-year-old to a football match on a windy, cold, rainy day and standing on the sidelines, smiling as if you're enjoying yourself.

Love is the process, always the process, in work and in life. I don't believe in having an awful time producing a television program that may ultimately be successful.

For me the process has to be nourishing, exciting, stimulating, exhilarating. Even the boring bits, and there are always boring bits.

Love is a gigantic embrace of life and lives, whether they are our intimates or not.

ROSALIND PRICE

Rosalind Price is a publisher of books for children and teenagers with Allen & Unwin. She was born in England, grew up in Kenya, and has made her home in Australia since 1979. She reads a lot, and does as much travelling, walking, cycling, gardening and singing as she can.

The challenge is to connect – with other people and ways of being, and with the natural world. You're less likely to harm a person or defile a place if you think of them as part of yourself. And you can't understand someone else until you know yourself. So I believe we should delve into ourselves as deeply and honestly as we can, and leap out into the world – as far and fearlessly as possible – to transcend our littleness.

My beliefs aren't fixed; they're tentative, exploratory, because life is paradoxical. We crave freedom but we need to belong. We chase happiness and light, but learn more from the dark, difficult places. We yearn for permanence, but are renewed by change. The ugliest thing has its own strange beauty. This contradictory nature of things calls for balance, for an agile response to complexity, a tolerance of difference and ambiguity. Life is too subtle to yield to one interpretation. The answer to important questions is often yes and no and maybe. The world suffers from dogmatic faith, which is often misused to exonerate, exclude or oppress. People without doubts are tiresome or dangerous.

So far, I have encountered no gods, loving, wrathful or capricious. Life itself is the thing, quite magnificent and mysterious enough without gods. It's life that calls for our reverence. And at the heart of life is connection. Everything is made of the same stuff. Consciousness – our delight and our torment – creates a sense of *us* and *other*, but ultimately we're all part of a great inexorable continuity.

My experience has been that there's more to love and celebrate in life than to fear or condemn, and that the very act of living by this assumption improves the balance. It's better to trust – in full knowledge of deceit, malice and indifference – than to arm against the worst. Trust and fear are both contagious. The tone of your voice influences the response you get, so take care to speak with warmth and respect. It may be temperament and circumstance that allow one person to be optimistic and another cynical, but there's also an element of choice, an act of will or faith.

The people I admire are those who give their full attention; the ones with an appetite for life, who look and listen and wonder, and acknowledge what they don't know. They treat everyone as a fellow human being (even in the bank, at immigration, or in conflict). They value beauty and authenticity. They're serious-minded and playful. They laugh a lot. They tussle with ideas and hunt for meaning, with a keen sense of the absurd. They're at home in their own skin. They make art in any way they can. They may do this cooking a meal, digging a hole, tending a child or writing a novel. They may be unobtrusive or flamboyant. But they have a vital attitude of heart and mind, and a respect for people and place, for tools and techniques, for process rather than product.

I also believe: Bicycles are better than cars. We should design our cities to encourage the best kinds of human interaction, not traffic. We must choose to retain wild places, whatever the cost. There's more honour in forgiveness than vengeance. The straight road is seldom the most interesting. You're lucky if you find a passion, to direct your energies. Reason without emotion is stupid; emotion without reason is careless. Busyness can be a way of avoiding oneself. Friendship is more durable than romance. Our most selfless love is for our children. Music is the purest form of expression and connection; nothing has such delicate power to pierce our defences and open us up to beauty. Tea is better than coffee. You should put the lid on the toothpaste, and tap the pointy end of a boiled egg. And Australia needs Radio National.

THÉRÈSE RADIC

Dr Thérèse Radic is a Melbourne based musicologist, playwright and biographer. As a musicologist she specialises in Australian music history and has been a pioneer in her field. She has published widely in this area and is currently completing a history of Australia's colonial music. Her biographies include *Bernard Heinze*; *Melba; the Voice of Australia*; and *G.W.L. Marshall-Hall*. Her published and produced plays include *Some of My Best Friends are Women*, *A Whip Round for Percy Grainger*, *Madame Mao*, *Peach Melba* and *The Emperor Regrets*. With *Madame Mao* she began the Chinese trilogy, which she recently completed with *Shanghai Sisters* and *George and the Dragon*, both of which are in development with Melbourne's Playbox Theatre Company. In March 2004 the National Library published Dr Radic's edited diaries of F.S. Kelly, expatriate Australian composer-pianist, Olympic gold medalist and World War One hero who was killed in action on the Somme at thirty-five.

I find the concept of belief, of accepting a thing as true, of the notion of faith in the rightness of a course of action, difficult and it's this that seems central to what has been asked of me here. I can't quite bring myself to trust both my own judgment and the judgment of others. I am not so much a disbeliever as a distruster. Maybe it's because my parents were country people come to the city in the Depression who somehow seemed to be a generation behind everyone else in their view of the world. Maybe it was the distrust of working class Footscray where I grew up, where Catholic Micks (I was baptised Maureen Thérèse O'Halloran) literally fought hard to make ends meet and where underworld celebrities kept the rest of us silent when questioned. You didn't trust anyone and the truth was flexible. Fear was a fact of life. Maybe it was the war that shadowed my childhood with its fears of invasion, its saving ways and its rationing, the uncle at the fall of Singapore and in Changi, the women of the family clinging to the radio for news, and their hidden weeping, mother, sister, sweetheart, me. Who do you believe in a world like that? What do you believe in? Maybe it was the Catholic boarding school that took my teenage years and educated us to be nuns, or wives procreating as God willed and not us. By then my dad had made it into the world of the slightly moneyed, via the sale of black market petrol during the war and junk after it. My mother wanted me to be a lady, hence schooling across town where I would be less contaminated by the place where I was born and the life outside our front door. The Micks were coming up in the world and were shortly to change its attitudes and its politics with me swept up in it, riding the crest of a wave of post-war prosperity, Commonwealth scholarships that gave us careers and influence, and the cracking open of the solidarity of our peculiar brand of socialism as we began to question the church that governed our every move. That's what education will do for you. We married young. We took a ship to see the Old World, we came home to put our ideals to the test when we found that the Old World excluded us and we didn't care. And then the whole world changed again, this time spinning not against the girls with wedding bands and ambitions, but towards us, me and the other good girls who were falling out with faith in God's will and the church's implacability over contraception in the first days of the Pill. It was still arguable whether we had souls and as for our bodies, well! We walked out. Out of the church, out of our ancestral faith, out of our marriages, questioning even that, the sanctity of marriage. Feminism, for a time, was what I believed in, female liberty, equality, sorority. But this, too, passed as we got older, richer and more self-absorbed, we who were now the makers of a country's destiny. If there is anything I believe in now it's the power of doubt. It prompts endless questions of those who still want to speak in my name, tell me what to do, what to think. Two questions preoccupy me these days, in this secular society with its fading moral sense, this democracy in crisis: who are you who will not allow me to pay my debt to this place that has so long fostered me, a debt owed to those from whom it was stolen? Who are you to imprison children in my name, the children of the terrified come to me for help? And there's that other nagging question, how did I come to this place where I allow others to dictate such terms out

of fear? If I believe in the necessity of the questioning then I must not only find but implement
the answers, if I and my country are to amount to
anything.

DIMITY REED

Dimity Reed graduated in architecture from the University of Melbourne and ran her own architecture practice before joining RMIT University as Professor of Urban Design. She is a Life Fellow of the Royal Australian Institute of Architects and writes extensively on architecture, urban design and cities in the press and in professional journals. Her book, *Tangled Destinies – the National Museum of Australia*, was published in 2002 and she is a contributor to *Judging Architecture; Issues, Divisions, Triumphs*, published in November 2003. She is a Trustee of the Shrine of Remembrance and a board member of the Urban and Regional Land Corporation and Zoos Victoria. She is the City of Melbourne's Ambassador for Architecture and has been closely involved with the development of Melbourne's Docklands since 1987.

I believe that the world has always been a difficult place, filled with starvation, bitter conflict and terrible unfairness. So, against the advice of many, I am reluctant to think that this age we live in is particularly dreadful – only that the ills appear more prevalent and shocking because we are witness to them on screens and in newspapers every day.

Our medieval forebears living in a village thirty miles from an evil Inquisition would have sown and gathered their crops unaware of the terror, and concerned only to produce enough food to ensure the survival of their family until the next sunrise. But now we know within minutes when nine hundred people die in an overfilled ferry, when an entire village is wiped out by neighbours who believe in another god, or when a child walks into a school with a loaded rifle and ends the lives of classmates.

And the danger in seeing and hearing so much horror is that it can deaden our sense of being of use, of being able to help.

I believe that optimism is essential; we have to believe that we can make things better in some way, that our shock and concerns can be turned into actions which can contribute to solutions.

Pessimism is self defeating; no situation has ever been improved by seeing it as unchangeable.

Hope is essential. I believe it is the one quality that has caused the human race to survive. Throughout history, and in our own time no less, people have given birth in wartime, in famine and in drought, and have protected the new life with a determination that could seem to outsiders to surpass good sense. They have suffered terrible deeds and survived, because they believed that *life could get better*. Intrinsic to our shared humanity is the belief that there is a future, and that future can probably be better than the present.

The world is filled with infinite possibilities which are hanging in the air all around us, waiting to be plucked, explored, acted on and enjoyed. One of my favourite writers, a very funny Englishman, Alan

Bennett, said that life is rather like a tin of sardines and that we're all looking for the key. I think it is worth looking everywhere in our search for that key and to venture bravely into unknown places because these ventures can tell us much about ourselves, the people we meet, and the complex world that we all live in. I suspect that we each only understand events and ideas that have somehow collided with our own lives, and unless we give ourselves every opportunity to encounter those collisions – those people who lead different lives, think and know different things – we are in danger of our minds closing shut like clam shells on a beach.

And, importantly, the adventures make for an entertaining life.

I want to say something about money. We live in an age in which money has achieved a celebrity quite beyond its intrinsic worth; it is talked about and aspired to so that it has now become a sort of character in society, like Mickey Mouse. The Poet, Carl Sandburg, wrote that: 'Money buys everything except love, personality, freedom, immortality, silence, and peace'. Money can buy everything, indeed, except those things that humanity has always believed are worth dying for. So, place no faith in money and be wary of its cousin, discontent.

Friends and family are the best of things. It is the value we place on the domestic affections which underpin the way we value the bigger world.

MATTHEW REILLY

At age thirty, Matthew Reilly is the author of six novels, including *Ice Station*, *Scarecrow* and *Hover Car Racer*. His books are sold in twenty countries, in eighteen languages.

THE DAY I GOT A KICK UP THE ARSE

I did pretty well at high school. I think I came sixth in my year in Year 12, which, when you consider all the sport I played, wasn't bad at all. Now I'm no genius or anything, but I do have a pretty good 'reading memory' – not quite photographic, but close. That said, I've always worked hard, put my head down and given myself every chance to succeed – at school, at sport, in life.

In all of those fields – school, sport, life – I've encountered others who were heaps more talented than I was, more naturally gifted, and more materially 'advantaged' (read: they had wealthy parents). And I've seen those same people waste their talents, squander their gifts, and piss away their advantaged upbringing. And so sometimes I wonder why I – and not they – have this *drive* to achieve, this primal urge to move ever *forward*, to actually use whatever capabilities I've been given.

Thing is, I wasn't born with this drive. I learned it. But where?

I trace it to a conversation I had with my best mate, a guy named John Schrooten, late in my first year at university. You see, after I did all right at school, I went to Law School (as you do), and there – let's be honest – I didn't get the marks I'd been used to. I was cruising. Doing enough to get Credits, sure (and quite happy getting Credits), but generally enjoying the freedom of university life.

And then I spoke to my mate, John, about how we were doing in our respective courses (he was doing a Bachelor of Business at another uni). He heard about my marks and he frowned. 'Matt,' he said. 'Can I say something seriously?'

Like most Australian males, I hardly ever talk seriously with anyone, so when my best mate suggested it, I paid attention. 'Sure,' I said.

What he said next floored me.

He said, 'Matt. You're a smart guy. A lot smarter than I am. I'll never be able to get the marks you can get – but if I *could* get those kinds of marks, I would. You *can* do really well at uni, so you *should* do well at uni.'

It was, in short, a gigantic kick up the arse.

Now, usually, it's your parents who give you a kick up the arse – so naturally you ignore them. But when it's a friend – someone your own age, with the same experiences – who says something like that, it hits hard.

And so I worked harder at Law School, and five

years later, I walked out of there with a Distinction average. During that same period (to the complete incomprehension of some of my fellow law students) I wrote a couple of action novels – which would later be picked up by a publisher.

Now, the publication of those books has meant that I've never practised law. But I've never regretted going to Law School or working as hard as I did there. Law School taught me discipline – of thought as well as practice. I learned how to structure my thinking; to look at the world in a questioning, analytical way. I also learned *to always do my best*. I throw all of these things into the writing of my novels, and it's now my novels that give me such enormous pleasure in life. But I might not have done any of this had John not given me that talking-to.

And so, in the end, what I've discovered is, thanks to a song by Pink: *you get what you're given, it's all how you use it.*

You might have rocket-scientist brains. You might have model good looks. You might have grown up with money. But if you don't *use* those gifts, then you're nothing.

(As an interesting aside, if you examine the heroes in my novels, especially Shane Schofield in *Ice Station* and Jason Chaser in *Hover Car Racer*, you'll find that they are somewhat talented people, but not super-duper gifted. The *villains* are super-gifted – it's my heroes who beat them through sheer bloody-minded determination.)

I have a few brains, not lots but some, and back

then I also had something else working for me – a good friend who was gutsy enough to tell me to get off my butt and use them.

Oh, and what happened to John? He got his Bachelor of Business and is now a very highly sought-after executive in the Sydney business world. Not really surprising, is it?

Eric Rolls

Eric Rolls began his public career at the age of five telling stories before an adult audience. His first published work, the poem *Death Song of a Mad Bush Shepherd*, was written when he was fifteen. Twenty books and many hundreds of articles and essays on diverse topics have followed. His work appears in newspapers, journals and anthologies both in Australia and overseas.

In 1991 he was made a member of the Order of Australia (AM) for services to literature and environmental awareness. He is an honorary Doctor of the University at the University of Canberra and a Fellow of the Australian Academy of the Humanities.

The Creed that I Decreed

A life is not lived that is not celebrated. How else do you give thanks for being alive? Whom do you thank? I do not believe in a god who oversees the trivialities of individuals; I believe in a massive intelligence who organised the universes.

The concept of original sin seems to me to be a major sin, it derogates one of the glories of life. Reproduction is the most certain indicator of a creative authority. No matter where they fit or what their duties are, the absolute compulsion of every plant and animal is to reproduce. Who but a master planner would have thought of combining compelling need with exquisite sensation?

There are three menus for living, so inextricably involved it is impossible to put them in order. They are making love, eating and drinking, and making absolute use of one's talents.

It was once thought that only human beings understood the consequence of sexual union. The more I learn the more it seems that every living thing understands it. The invisible cells of budding yeasts of the *Saccharomyces* genus (one of the species is used in bread-making) choose their partners according to the strength of a pheromone signal. They actively seek improvement, it is not a chemical accident.

Food and wine are an essential element of the wonderful life I lived with Joan, my first wife. It lifted us out of the mediocrity of the 1950s. Food carries the same wonderment, it demands the same intensity of imaginative preparation, as sex. When Elaine came the wonder increased since we added all sorts of Asian and Italian dishes to our lovemaking. Available ingredients were changing with the population. And the planning of *A Celebration of Food and Wine* took us on trips through Australia and overseas. Everything we ate and drank carried the added flavour of words.

Food needs touch as much as a woman, as much as I need it. I am currently massaging salt, sugar, pepper and chopped dill into a slab of raw salmon to make gravlax for Christmas visitors. The kitchen is not a factory, a workshop of gadgets, it is the hub of the home, the source of joyful life. The smells emanating from it attract the senses from all over the house. It is where sustenance is created, health, respect, comfort, excitement, expectation, satisfaction, wonder, imagination. There is always excitement in opening a bottle of wine. What I release is a cool morning ten, fifteen, twenty years ago. I open history and a profound factory of chemicals of wondrous taste and smell.

Making use of talents, so much an obligation, is difficult. I began telling my own stories in public when I was five years old. Later, when I was a farmer as well as a storyteller, I wrote poetry. That fitted in with working the farm. But when I decided to write history, when I left my wife and children on the farm while I went off to do a few weeks research at the Mitchell Library, even my mother was appalled. I should not do such a thing – my duty lay with my family. She did not understand at all that my first duty lay with my talents: I was here to write. And *They All Ran Wild*, the first big book, opened up a remarkable life for my whole family. Our lives became unexpected. Soon we were all going off on research together.

Most important of all is a belief in oneself. How else do you function as you know you ought to function?

LEANNE ROWE

Dr Leanne Rowe is a General Practitioner, National Chairman of the Royal Australian College of General Practitioners, Senior Lecturer at the Department of General Practice at the University of Melbourne and author of the book *What To Do When Your Children Turn Into Teenagers* (published by Doubleday in 2003). She was awarded 'Best Individual Contribution to Health Care in Australia' by the Australian Medical Association for her work with disadvantaged young people at Clockwork Young People's Health Service in Geelong. She has published two other books for teenagers – *Urgent* and *Girl X Recreated*.

My country rotation as a medical student was overshadowed by a heated argument between the GP and his wife. She was 'sacrificing her life in this hole of a place' and angrily stormed out to visit her children at their boarding school in Melbourne. One quarter of a century later, I look back at the experiences in general practice that made me feel like storming out or giving up:

Being ignored in the street by the sister of someone I reported for child abuse. Remaining professional when my child was victimised at school by one of my patients. Being called out to a cardiac arrest in the middle of lunch with best friends, whom I had not seen for a few years. A knock at the door at 2 am by a tearful, teenage boy who requested the morning-after pill for his girlfriend, as the condom broke twenty minutes before and 'her father would kill him'. Listening to my baby screaming for a breastfeed while I was resuscitating a choking child, who was rushed to my home by his parents. Having my supermarket shopping prolonged by a patient who asked my advice about his haemorrhoids. Taking my children on a long-awaited outing and stopping at a motor car accident, where instead they were entertained by fire engines, police, ambulances and a helicopter, unsupervised in the back of my car. Stopping at the next accident and praying I wouldn't know the family this time. Unbandaging my neighbour's hand at my kitchen table at 11 pm and finding that he amputated his finger, when he fell off the haystack that morning. ('Well, who else was going to milk the cows?') Trying desperately but unsuccessfully to resuscitate a teenage boy after an accident in the Main Street in front of his mother. Having to counsel a community's grief when you feel you can't contain your own . . .

Then I remind myself of so many other stories of courage and resilience in the face of chronic illness, child abuse, family breakdown and death. These are mostly the rich images of younger and older people who have taught me what my work requires of me beyond my work, and about the rewards of hanging in there for the long haul:

Receiving a letter of thanks from the abused child

who is now a thriving adult. Catching a glimpse of my neighbour on another lonely drive home from work: the sixty-five-year-old farmer riddled with arthritis (the day after being discharged from hospital for repair of his amputated finger), carrying a heavy bag of hay on his bent-over back to his beloved cows. Sharing a tearful moment with the mother who lost her son years ago in the Main Street accident, and feeling like my work is more valuable than gold. And because parenting is more difficult and wonderful than any of this, most of all it's the image of my eighteen-year-old son (who has previously noted that I am an overly anxious, ageing woman with a weird sense of humour and a big arse), saying to his careers advisor: 'I want to be just like my mum'.

MARGARET SCOTT

Margaret Scott was born in the English city of Bristol in 1934. After reading English at Cambridge, she worked in a false eyelash factory, taught in two schools and in 1959, emigrated to Tasmania with her first husband and their sixteen-month-old son. Although she arrived determined to return to Britain after two years, she is now addicted to Tasmania and would not live anywhere else. For twenty-four years she taught in the English Department of the University of Tasmania, retiring in 1989 to become a full-time writer.

Margaret has produced four books of poetry: *Tricks of Memory*, *Visited*, *The Black Swans* and *Collected Poems*; a collection of stories, essays and poems, *Changing Countries*; and two novels, *Family Album* and *In the Shadows*, which was first published as *The Baby Farmer*. With Vivian Smith, she edited *Effects of Light: The Poetry of Tasmania*. In 1997 Margaret wrote *Port Arthur: A Story of Strength and Courage* in response to the massacre which took place there in 1996. She has also written numerous articles, poems and short stories for periodicals in Australia, New Zealand, UK and the US, and a television script for Artist Services. She is a well-known public speaker and has appeared and debated on many television programs.

I would like to believe in a god or gods but, although I admire some people, like Frank Brennan, who have a strong religious faith, I can't locate in the vastness of the universe any being who cares about Earth's suffering children. Some who see things differently and are sure they are carrying out their god's will are all too ready to kick aside man-made laws and turn on each other, spreading death and misery across the world in the manner of Osama bin Laden or George W. Bush. So I think of the inhabitants of our planet as left to their own devices like passengers in a life-boat, adrift on a darkling sea.

If no god is guiding us, no supreme power has declared one set of human beings superior to others, so I believe we all have equal rights to draw rations according to, at least, our basic needs, as well as a duty to look out for one another and help keep the boat afloat. But, unlike Marx, I also believe that human needs are immensely complex and various, so that tyrannies grow up when leaders treat us as economic or political units with no hunger for imaginative or aesthetic experience, no hopes of knowing love or flashes of joy.

Most of my other beliefs flow from these convictions. I'm fairly green, for instance, because I believe that future generations have as much right as our own to a planet that hasn't been wrecked by pollution and still contains ancient forests and wild tigers. I also believe that the human spirit can draw nourishment from the natural world. Now that emphysema prevents me moving much, I'm sustained by looking out each day on forested hills and an ever-changing sea.

I'm sustained still more by the generosity and love of my family, friends and small community which make me glad to be aboard the life-boat. But nowadays I'm saddened by news of the wider world, especially the way Australia's leaders, playing on greed and fear, have made us a mean-spirited nation. We accept, with hardly a murmur, revelations of our leaders' lies and seem to believe that everyone will lie to get their way. So we refuse to listen to stories of suffering told by asylum-seekers or the Stolen Generation, refuse to be conned into opening our borders or our hearts or saying 'sorry' to those deprived of their birth-right. Instead we swallow the pseudo-rational lies which have come to pollute most regions of the world: money is the measure of all things; institutions set up to serve the common good are businesses which exist to turn a profit.

Australia's universities are a case in point. Reduced to vocational training colleges they are expected now to train students to earn big money. Users, of course, must pay for this privilege. Yet I believe that schools and universities, well staffed and well equipped, should be open to us all, free of charge, not only to train us to do work our society needs but to help us become better citizens and neighbours, partners and parents. At its best education can enhance our pleasure in the arts and intellectual enquiry; train us to think clearly – and, I hope, honestly – and promote informed debate in our communities. This was the vision of the Whitlam years. It has faded now but when Adam and Jarrah drop by I glimpse it again.

Adam has chosen to train not as a marketing manager but as an infant teacher. Jarrah has spent the summer in Oregon, working in a camp for disabled children. Both are eighteen. Their eyes shine, their favourite word is 'awesome', I believe their kind may have a chance of helping Australia slough off its cancerous growths of fear and greed.

Vincent Serventy

Vincent Serventy is a veteran of sixty years in the conservation movement, and thirty-six of those years have been spent as president of Australia's oldest conservation society, the Wild Life Preservation Society of Australia. He helped found many conservation groups, including WWF Australia, and Greening Australia. He is the Chairman of the NSW Nature Conservation Council.

He has written millions of words on nature and its conservation, published more than seventy books, and has made fifty documentaries for television.

He has been awarded a Doctorate of Science from Macquarie University for seminal work in education, conservation, and some avenues of science. His achievements include the adoption of the Wildlife Preservation Society's motto 'humans must learn to live in harmony within nature' by the World Conservation Union, the most influential association of its kind in the world.

Vincent Serventy also initiated the world's first Conservation Day; and the adoption of wildlife corridors, which are used today to save wildlife and to counter global warming. He has had much joy of the Earth with his wife, who has not only been a partner in his achievements, but also has some surpassing his own.

Since I was a teenager I had a passion to communicate with fellow humans. First with words; then images, adding photographs, black and white, then colour, numbering in their hundreds of thousands.

Movies came next, many kilometres of film for television documentaries. Then the human voice – I gave lectures galore, first in Great Britain, then on cruise ships. In America, always talking to conservation groups. Once I spoke to 6,000 in Scotland.

My early years were spent on a farm in the West Australian Darling Ranges near Perth. We eight children ran barefoot like brumbies across the hills. One memory is of lying in a field of pink everlastings, summer scented. And always the smell of gum leaves.

Then we moved nearer Perth for education with four hundred hectares of bushland nearby in King's Park. In the distance was the tower of the Great Hall of the University of Western Australia, a target for the future. Writing was in my blood. At fourteen I began a newspaper, with the family a built-in circulation.

Four years later sport occupied my leisure. Then, at university, during a second degree, my professor of Education suggested all his students should develop a philosophy of life.

I chose pragmatic realism. Accept what you can achieve at the time, always keeping your eyes on future goals. Radical in politics, I became President of the Labor Club, with Bob Hawke on my council.

Then an American couple came, wanting a guide for a month in the bush to search for the world's most primitive ant. Who better as a guide than myself?

Caryl Haskens was a mature man; later I discovered he was a millionaire, son of the founder of General Electric, but from my point of view more famous as the author of a classic work, *Of Ants and Men*.

He showed how ants had become agriculturists, slavemakers, communists. In Western Australia an Argentine ant invasion had destroyed the old enmity between clans, distinguished by a different odour. Soon they numbered millions, a major pest, until destroyed by insecticides.

Caryl also showed that ants had the same moral codes as humans; caring for their young, protecting the clan, taking injured companions back to the nest. His point was that all social organisms evolved those codes, otherwise their society fragments.

I told Caryl ants had no Moses, bringing the Ten Commandments, gently suggesting that was why I had no time for organised religion, only accepting nature as my guide.

My next major international visitor was Gro Harlem Brundtland, prime minister of Norway, who had chaired a UN committee to draw up the Environmental Bill of Rights to complement the 1948 Human Bill of Rights.

What use are human rights if you are a Japanese peasant dying from mercury poisoning caught from fish in the bay? Or dying from asbestosis caught in the Pilbara mines where you earned your daily bread? Or a Lapland mother finding danger has come from the atomic disaster in Chernobyl in far-off Russia?

'There is danger in the air you cannot smell or feel but our reindeer milk we cannot sell', Brundtland had written in a book, *Our Common Future*. It also contained twenty-nine principles to form the legal guides for a World Court. I used those beliefs in a new book, *Saving the World*, with the first principle coming from a poem read to a packed audience in a Perth Town Hall: my plea to save the jarrah forest from bauxite mining.

I took Martin Luther King's 'I have a dream', changing it to 'We have a dream', since in a democracy it is groups which move us forward. My first line was 'Of a world as part of nature we live in harmony within it.'

I took Brundtland's report and edited the twenty-nine legal principles into nine. Judith Wright, the great poet and patron of our society, suggested adding the need for a value system. The book became subtitled 'The ten green commandments'. Here they are:

1. All people have a right to an earth where they can live in good health to enjoy a fair quality of life.
2. No nation has the right to change the world of nature in a way that will damage the world's resources.
3. All nations must keep the present diversity of the natural world; its plants and animals and the beauty of its landscapes.

4. All nations must use their resources in a sustainable way, planning for a future when the supplies of oil and coal run out.
5. All nations giving aid must ensure this will increase the quality of life of those to whom help is given.
6. All resources which the world holds in common must be used for the common good.
7. All nations must carry out common agreements, abiding by the decisions of the World Court.
8. All nations must check their own environment's warning of dangers ahead.
9. All nations must develop a sustainable population policy, not expecting other nations to accept their excess due to unwise planning.
10. All nations must educate their people into a new morality which cares, not only for the rights of people, but also for the rights of the environment.

To which I would now add, 'If you need a religion, accept the religion of nature'.

When I come to die I will be satisfied, accepting Thoreau's words, 'I have lived'. Carol and I have been fortunate in our Darbyshire-Serventy genes, linking us with the past, ensuring our long life.

We have been fortunate in our partnership, with our lives devoted to nature; as well, museums are an important part of Carol's work. We have been fortunate in our partnership and our children, yet always we made our own luck.

I am working now on my last book, and bringing three older ones up to date because of remarkable new discoveries: *The Easy Guide to Green Living*; *Saving Australia* and *Saving the World*, under a new title *Saving Yourself: Australia and the World*.

Man Chien Shih

Venerable Man Chien Shih was born in a small province named Tao Yuan, in Taiwan. Since a young age she has had a strong interest in finding out what life is all about.

In order to search for the truth, she joined the Fo Guang Shan Buddhist Order in 1987 as a student in the Fo Guang Shan Tsung Lin University and was ordained in 1988 under Master Hsing Yun of the Fo Guang Shan Buddhist Order in Taiwan.

Venerable Man Chien possesses a deep sense of compassion and a full-hearted commitment to pursue her spiritual growth. Her brave steps in following humanistic Buddhism have always been an inspiration to her Dharma brothers and sisters.

Venerable Man Chien is talented in many areas, including literature and the arts. She has led the Nan Tien Temple in New South Wales from a newly established monastery to a temple highly recognised by the general public.

Due to her intelligence and strong devotion, she has been able to shoulder important responsibilities for the Fo Guang Shan Buddhist Order for the past fifteen years. She has been Assistant Director-General of the Fo Guang Shan Buddhist Order in Taiwan, Abbess of many Fo Guang Shan Buddhist Temples, including New South Wales, Melbourne, Christchurch and Auckland, and is currently Minister for Fo Guang

Shan Temples in Australia and New Zealand, and Dean of
the Fo Guang Shan Tsung Lin University in Taiwan.

In today's society, as everything is constantly evolving, different needs arise, and we strive to meet
those needs.

Humanistic Buddhism can help us in everyday
living. I believe this. Here are a few ideas taught by
Venerable Master Hsing Yun on how a person in this
world can live a carefree and meaningful life.

Be a mirror to yourself
Most people only see the faults of others but never
see their own shortcomings. How can you change
your bad habits, and change for the better if you can't
see yourself? If you always contemplate on your
actions and speech, you will be more aware of how
to improve your mannerisms.

Be a briefcase, pick up and let go at ease
When you need a briefcase, you pick it up. When
you no longer need it, you put it aside. The briefcase
you hold on to when you no longer need it becomes
a burden. On the other hand, if you cannot find the
briefcase when you need it, it is a great inconveni-
ence. Therefore, you should take yourself seriously
when the circumstances demand it, but let go when
the need no longer arises. In doing this you will be
truly free.

Be a paintbrush, beautify and improve life
Paintbrushes can be used to create beautiful images and impressive pictures. Likewise in your life, you can use your capabilities to enhance your life, thereby enriching yourself.

If you see a person who scolds you, or always take you for granted, instead of disliking them, you can think of them as your teacher – a teacher of patience and tolerance.

Be a notebook, record all your successes and failures
A notebook is used for recording purposes. You should conduct yourself similarly by honestly recording everything you have done, whether successful or otherwise. Then you need to assess yourself, encourage or give yourself credit when it is due.

Be a candle, brighten up others' lives
A person should never be self-centred and selfish. You should apply empathy and put yourself in others' shoes. A candle is burned to brighten our lives. Compassion is the foundation of an altruistic philosophy.

Be a clock, keep track of time and cherish every moment
The clock ticks away every minute of the day from hour to hour in an orderly fashion. Once a day has passed, it will never return. This serves as a reminder for you to cherish every minute, so that you may value your life and realise your potential.

★

You cannot control the world, or change the world to suit your needs. But you can change your attitude to see life in a more carefree and meaningful way, thus changing your life in a positive manner.

ANNETTE SHUN WAH

As a child Annette Shun Wah dreamt of becoming a glamorous, kung fu fighting secret agent. She's had to make do with being a television and radio personality, AFI nominated actor and award-winning author. She currently produces *The Movie Show* on SBS-TV.

NO REGRETS

I knew about regret long before I knew what it was called. Before I understood how a regret formed, and what its purpose was in life. In a family whose heart was heavy with yearning, regret settled in as a permanent lodger.

My father was a poultry farmer in the back blocks of Brisbane, but he'd wished for so much more. Born in central Queensland, he'd completed only two years of schooling before his family relocated to Hong Kong, going 'back' to the land of our ancestors. He was intelligent and good with his hands. As a child he spent his spare time painstakingly crafting model planes and dreaming of one day taking to the skies. Despite his limited schooling, at the age of eighteen he secured an apprenticeship as an aircraft mechanic. But before he'd taken even one step on that journey, Japanese bombers descended on

Kowloon. It was December 1941. By Christmas Day
Hong Kong had fallen and my father's dreams were
shattered.

'I could have been an aircraft mechanic.' Whenever he told you that he said it with such certainty,
as if it were proof of his potential for greatness. Being
a poultry farmer, toiling from morning to night
scratching together a living, didn't cut it.

My mother was a seamstress in Hong Kong. I have
a copy of her passport photo taken shortly before
she boarded the steam-ship to Australia, to marry
my father. Eager to leave the crowded, poverty-
stricken streets of Hong Kong behind, her eyes gaze
defiantly into the camera, full of hope. She should
have looked into a crystal ball instead. Perhaps then
she'd have seen the lifetime of hard work, loneliness
and isolation that would grind down her optimism.

Whether it took the shape of an opportunity
missed or an opportunity that should never have
been taken, regret haunted my family like a hungry
ghost, gobbling up the achievements of the interven-
ing years as if they didn't count, leaving a clear view
all the way back to what might have been. I vowed at
an early age never to give myself cause for regret.

Of course it's not possible to live entirely without
regret, just as it's not possible to avoid the unpre-
dictability of fate. But much of the time, we do have
some choice in how we steer our destinies.

When I was nineteen I was offered a job as a radio
producer. I had hardly any qualifications and absolutely no experience. My parents advised against it.

I was midway through a Social Work degree. I would have to forgo a scholarship that supported me through my studies and guaranteed a job at the end. But now I was standing at the open door to my favourite radio station; a station I covertly tuned in to every night, eavesdropping on a world so removed from my own that I had never imagined I could visit let alone reside there. I pictured myself at my parents' age, mouthing the words, 'I could have been a radio producer' and a chill ran through me.

I banished the cautionary ghost of regret and plunged headlong into a media career. It was the one 'lucky break' from which everything else has flowed – radio, television, feature film, acting, writing.

You know, I could have been a social worker, and about that, I have no regrets.

BRUCE SMEATON

Bruce Smeaton is largely self-taught and probably the first Australian composer to support himself solely by composition. Prolific, eclectic and experimental, he has composed music for over 2000 television and radio commercials, won a Best Pop Instrumental, five AFI Awards, and scored sixty-five feature films and television series besides much chamber and orchestral music, a ballet and countless other works. He has worked and recorded in London, Los Angeles and Mexico City as well as Australia. Fourteen recordings of his film music have been issued. He still composes, writes articles and short stories and restores small French voiturettes of the early-1920s. He is very happy.

I believe passionately in reform; ongoing, rational, wide-reaching reform that benefits all sections of Australian society. Australia has always been an unfair society but the mix changes with time. You don't go to the doctor to tell them how well you feel and you cannot discuss reform without appearing negative, because you are talking about correcting the sicknesses in our society rather than celebrating the best that Australia has to offer. Not everyone relishes reform but the gap between the haves and have-nots has widened in the last twenty years. It must not only be stopped, but reversed. At one level this is easy and at another extremely difficult. For example, the rich, the powerful, the successful, and the famous rarely want to change the system that they think has made them rich, powerful, successful and famous, while conservatives are of that mind because they like things as they are. The following are thought-starters culled from a list I've been accumulating as things occur to me.

Government
Zero tolerance of any rorting or corruption. Dismissal, loss of seat and privileges and automatic court action to determine an appropriate prison sentence with no loopholes in the legislation and the strictest guidelines for the presiding magistrate. Pay, superannuation, pensions and expenses to be brought into line with other parts of society; initiated and determined independent of politicians and public servants.

White collar crime
Abolish the artificial distinction between crimes of violence and corporate white-collar crimes, which should be a technical and legal distinction but no more. Nothing could be more violent than the actions of white-collar criminals who can, and have, ruined the lives of thousands of people.

Culture

Culture cannot be imposed from above. Like grass, it grows from below. Fund individuals and groups but only for a maximum of, say, fifteen years. If the funded individual or group has failed to discover an audience, a market or personal expression within this time public funding automatically ceases.

Infrastructure

The infrastructure of this country has been run down for so long that the results have become a fact of life. If health, hospitals, transport, defence and community services are run down (which they are) what on earth are politicians doing with our taxes? The demise of manufacturing has been a disgrace through neglect, inappropriate change of ownership and asset-stripping.

Globalisation or free trade

Has it struck anyone else that the greatest supporters of free trade are those people least affected by the implementation of such a policy? Politicians, the legal profession, the medical profession, accountants, bankers and so on.

Professional status

Abolish the artificial classification of professional and non-professional, as it is meaningless today. Professionals have demonstrated convincingly over the years that many of them are no better educated, ethical or moral than any other section of the community.

Trucks on trains

Every month there are more trucks on the road and they're not getting any smaller. Most of the freight they carry should be carried, along with the trucks themselves, by train.

Speeding and drunk driving

Slower speeds don't always make for safer speeds. Italy has just increased the speed limit as research revealed that, in certain circumstances, slower speeds caused more serious accidents. Speeding fines should be calculated as a percentage of the offender's gross income and the fines imposed in two-week or one month increments depending on the seriousness of the offence.

Hard drugs

A free lifetime supply of drugs to any addict providing it is administered and not just handed over. In return, the addict turns his/her pusher in. This is much cheaper than the cost of playing cops and robbers. Identified, the addict is regularly available for counselling and other help.

Economics and incomes

Most things we want are made by someone else. The reward structure doesn't reflect this. Streamed incomes reflecting this interdependency should be the norm. Hospitals and doctors cannot function without nurses yet nurses are appallingly rewarded.

Corporate

No person should be permitted to serve as an executive of a firm or sit on a board without at least ten years working in that particular industry. No business involving food, or a non-renewable resource, may be sold to purchasers not resident in Australia.

Canberra

Gallipoli and the Western Front were dreadful enough but the biggest disaster in recent Australian history has been Canberra, and all because a whole bunch of pollies couldn't agree. I've read various estimates ranging from fifty billion up to three-hundred-billion spent to create a city that had no economic basis for its existence. Imagine how different Australia would be if that amount of money, whatever it is, had gone into hospitals, roads, research, manufacturing, universities, defence and anything else you can think of. It's too late to reverse this but we can try and make sure they don't do it again.

Our anthem

Advance Australia Fair is a rotten tune and does not reflect our view of ourselves. *Waltzing Matilda* is a terrific tune and suits us, which is why people keep on singing it. WM was adopted by Australians because it was a mirror that reflected an image of themselves they felt was appropriate. That is why it is known all over the world. Banjo Paterson's words could be used for informal occasions while new words could be written for ceremonial use. Overseas, every man and his dog thinks that WM is our national anthem. My choice to write new words would be Les Murray, a great poet, and a quintessential Australian.

ANNE SUMMERS

Anne Summers is a best-selling author and journalist who has had a long career in politics and the media. She is the author of several books, including the now classic *Damned Whores and God's Police*, which is still in print twenty-eight years after it was first published in 1975. Her most recent book is *The End of Equality*, published in 2003 by Random House. Her political background includes her time as a political adviser to Prime Minister Paul Keating prior to the 1993 federal elections. She ran the Office of the Status of Women, for Prime Minister Bob Hawke, from 1983 to 1986. Since 2000 she has been chair of the board of Greenpeace International. She is also Deputy President of Sydney's Powerhouse Museum.

I used to believe in the basic worthiness and decency of the people of this country but in recent years I have lost the faith.

I used to believe it was true that an Australian would 'give you the shirt off his back', that we were 'generous to a fault' and that we were indeed the land of the 'fair go'.

When I lived in New York in the late 1980s and early 1990s I used to compare the barracuda style of doing business there with my fond memories of simple Aussie trustworthiness where a hand-shake sealed a deal and a person was 'as good as their word'.

I bragged to American friends about our tolerance, our multiculturalism ('better than your melting-pot', I used to say), our generosity towards the shattered people of Kampuchea, our open arms welcome to Vietnamese boat people and how our Prime Minister cried when he announced, after the massacres around Tiananmen Square in 1989, that 20,000 Chinese students then in Australia would be granted permanent residence.

It's hard to believe that this was only fifteen years ago.

Since then, and more especially over the past seven years, we have become a brutal, selfish and unfair place whose national character seems to have altered in ways that are quite perplexing to those who believed these other traits were somehow ingrained in all of us.

Our most spectacular change of heart has, of course, been towards asylum seekers who have come across the seas to make Australia their home. Whereas once we embraced political refugees from Vietnam and Cambodia, in recent years we have turned away people from Iran, Iraq and Afghanistan and watched with cold dispassion while 352 frantic people drowned as their overcrowded vessel, known since as SIEV X, sank a few miles from our territory. In our indifference to the plight of people fleeing religious, political and economic persecution, we have spent billions on a spurious Pacific 'solution' while paying the bare minimum required to finance the work of the United Nations High Commission

for Refugees, a body that must deal with an historic-
ally high tide of human refuse awaiting in vain for
admission to the lands of the globally rich.

Those few thousand who managed to slip past
our patrols and reach our shores were denied our
embrace. Instead we herded them behind barbed
wire into concentrations camps located in some of
the most inhospitable parts of our harsh dry land,
then shielded our ears to their cries of misery.

Over the past decade Australian homeowners have
enjoyed unbelievable capital gains windfalls that have
made millionaires out of a multitude of ordinary
middle-class people. This new-found wealth seems
not to have enlarged our hearts or our consciences.
Few among us have sought to share our fortunes
with the globally dispossessed whose numbers are
increasing at an astounding rate. We share not our
shirts, we are not generous and we are no longer fair.

How did this happen, and will it ever change? It
requires a huge leap of faith to believe we can restore
those values that once made us a decent and worthy
place. I am ready to believe we *can* because so many
of us want it to happen. Do I believe we *will*? No,
I don't believe – but I do hope.

DON TALBOT

Don Talbot, OBE, BA (Hons), MA (Canada), is renowned internationally as the greatest swimming coach in the world, the man who led Australian swimming to new heights. Steering Australia to major successes at Olympic, World Championships and Commonwealth Games, Don's proudest moment was when Australian was crowned number one at the 2001 World Championships in Japan.

Don Talbot became Australia's Head Coach of Swimming in 1964, and retained that position until 1972, when, unhappy with the state of Australian swimming and its lack of funding, he moved to Canada. In 1974 he was appointed Head Coach of the Canadian Swim Team, and in 1988 he was appointed Executive Director of Canadian Swimming, and was twice named Canadian Coach of the Year.

Enticed to return to Australia in 1989, Don was appointed Head Coach and set about rebuilding Australian swimming. Introducing cameras and computers to analyse every stroke, touch and turn, Don took swimming high-tech in an endeavour to discover the fractions of seconds necessary to win. At the 2000 Olympic Games, Australia finished second to the US with five gold, nine silver and four bronze medals.

I believe in personal freedoms provided they do not offend, hurt, degrade, belittle or compromise others. In the early years of my life I did not ever give thought to what I believed in, except perhaps planning for good times, personal gratification, and generally playing as much as I could. Whatever came into my head, or whatever my friends suggested, I did. On reflection, I also didn't give much thought to my family and took them for granted because they were always there, whenever I needed them.

It wasn't until much later in my life – and it finally came to me with a jolt when I lost my older brother, who was closest to me – that I felt an insecurity which wasn't in my normal makeup. Insecurity is still there but more now as a shadow in my thoughts than something up front and threatening. My brother's loss made me very much aware of the role all my family had played in the achievements and freedoms of my life.

As I matured and my life experiences broadened, by way of extensive travel, both in Australia and abroad, my thoughts began to focus a great deal on life in Australia and how it compared with life in other countries. These thoughts simply surfaced from my subconscious, rather than by conscious effort on my part. While I was and still am impressed with what I have seen and experienced elsewhere in the world, I have come to the conclusion that there are very, very few countries where I would prefer to live; in fact I would rather spend my life here. Over the years I have lived in parts of the world for long periods, or have just visited many times, and they would easily be classed as having high socio-economic lifestyles, the sort of lifestyles that many people would dream to live. They are really not for me. I want to stay in Australia because we have here, at least for now, the opportunity to live those freedoms I mentioned at the beginning of this essay. However, this desire of mine could be thwarted; my wife, who is of another country by birth, may want to go home to live her last years. But to paraphrase another man's words, wherever I may be, I will always call Australia 'home'.

However, although I feel strongly about Australia, in very recent times there have been changes taking place that could threaten the personal freedoms we all enjoy. With almost instant global communication, low-cost world travel available to almost everyone, a reawakening of seemingly forgotten religions, but also significantly increased media intrusions into our lives, rapidly rising costs of living, skyrocketing home values and so on, it seems that our freedoms have been increased exponentially in many ways but more meaningfully, they are being taken from us. In particular, the individual is being forgotten in the name of 'security'. National and international wellbeing are the priorities now, which may not be a bad thing. However it is a bad thing if it comes as a cost to personal freedom. Poverty and the devaluation of chosen ways of living is on the increase – not on the decrease as most would have predicted from our increased knowledge and wealth.

People today seem less self-sufficient, less content than they were in my years of growing up. They look for more from governments, in fact demand it as a right. There seem to be many more people in personal trouble. Self-management skills have not been fostered and some turn to solving their life problems with drugs.

There also seems to be a greed and envy that we in Australia, and possibly the world too, have not experienced before. To even stay alive today seems to be at the cost of our fellow man. Governments and media and other agencies tell us via their propaganda of the good things created to make life easier. However, this is not the apparent result in Australia. Our freedoms – my freedoms – are being restricted and the many laws being introduced almost daily are giving us – me – less and less room to move.

Australian authorities are failing to show that simple respect and courtesy towards others and their needs will give us all a life with enjoyment and reward. Personal freedom does not come with more police, more military to watch over us.

I believe these freedoms can be ours again provided we all work together for them. Australia must review its policies, its laws, its expectations of its citizens and rethink what life should be about.

As life goes on, we all want it surely to be a full, comfortable, rewarding and worry-free experience. This is what I want, this is what I strive for, and this is what I believe can be achieved.

BARBARA THIERING

Dr Barbara Thiering has an international reputation in the field of the Dead Sea Scrolls and Christian Origins. She taught in the School of Divinity at Sydney University for twenty-two years, and in retirement is continuing research and publication.

Her main popular books are *Jesus the Man* (1992), *Jesus of the Apocalypse* (1995) and *The Book that Jesus Wrote* (1998), all published by Transworld-Doubleday (now Random House).

The effect of her close analysis of the New Testament, with the aid of new information from the Dead Sea Scrolls, is to show that Jesus was a human hero only, instrumental in the fusion of Roman culture with Judaism that took place in the 1st century AD.

Jesus the Man has been an international bestseller, translated into seven foreign languages. The controversy about its findings is still continuing.

NO RELIGION, ONLY FAITH

Fifty-five years ago I stood with a crowd of other first year undergraduates at a student house party, lustily singing with them:

And can it be, that I should gain
An interest in my Saviour's blood?
Died he for me, who caused his pain,
For me, who him to death pursued?

The tune was great, the ambience was great. I felt warm, part of a communal family with whom I belonged. If anyone had asked me, 'Do you really believe that blood can save you? Are you really so sinful that you pursued Jesus to his death?' I would have giggled nervously. Of course it was only a kind of poetry.

Still, in order to be a member of this warm hymn-singing community, we had to sign a doctrinal statement, affirming that we believed a list of things. They included the infallibility of the Bible, the virgin birth, the bodily resurrection of Jesus, the Second Coming. Long afterwards I learned that this list of 'fundamentals' of Christian belief had been drawn up only in 1909, in Chicago Illinois, in a series of tracts designed to counteract the growing influence of scientific thought. From the rich and varying languages for Christian faith, the fundamentalists had selected a set of what were declared to be facts, facts in the scientific sense. You had to believe them if you were a Christian, and if you didn't you were 'off the beam', a social pariah.

It took only another year or so of undergraduate study to make me question supernaturalism, but I still felt that there was something worth staying with. While completing my Arts degree I enrolled in an external Theology degree from London University. The books recommended opened my eyes to what was going on in the world's best theological circles. Discoveries of ancient documents in the 19th century, continuing in the 20th and culminating in the discovery of the Dead Sea Scrolls, gave new knowledge of the historical contexts within which past religious languages had been formed. So great is our distance from that past that to commit oneself to live intellectually in the 1st Century is, rather, to be a social pariah in our own time.

Belief is a very different thing from faith. Through all the subsequent years of research, in which I was able to contribute to scholarship on Christian origins and show how time-bound the beliefs were, I experienced no weakening of faith. The dictionary definition of faith, equating it with belief, is quite wrong. Faith has no content, there are no words for it. It is a state of mind, a buoyancy of spirit, a music that plays without language. From the internal well of faith comes personal balance, the energy to oppose what is destructive to oneself and others, the tenacity to keep going when everything seems to be against you.

Because faith is a product of the human capacity for survival, an understanding of it is found within all the great religions. There is a language for it in the mystical traditions of Christianity. Judaism had its own version of it, in its refusal to objectify God by a name or by images. Buddhism developed its language and the discipline of spiritual awareness further than did other religions.

Yet even the languages that free us from language are passing. They may be spoken for the moment, to move us beyond fixity of belief, but if they are held to be themselves a truth they attach us to a name, an institution. I would not want to use any name, or ally myself again with any defined religious group.

For me, all that survives of that rousing hymn is the question 'And can it be?'

CHARLES 'BUD' TINGWELL

In a distinguished career spanning more than sixty years, Bud Tingwell has acted and directed in film, theatre and television. An early start as an actor while still a schoolboy saw him featured in Jack Davey's *Billy Bunter* radio series. This was interrupted by World War Two during which he completed seventy-five operational missions as a photographic reconnaissance pilot in the Royal Australian Air Force. He fought the war again in his first Hollywood movie *The Desert Rats*, appearing with Richard Burton and James Mason, then returned to tour Australia in memorable productions of *Simon and Laura* and *The Deep Blue Sea* with Googie Withers and John McCallum. In 1956 he went to England for *The Shiralee* with Peter Finch.

Living in England with his family for sixteen years, Bud became a household name in the television series *Emergency Ward 10*, appeared opposite Dame Margaret Rutherford in four classic Miss Marple films and starred in *There's a Girl in My Soup* at the Comedy Theatre in London for two years.

Back in Australia he played the lead in the early television series *Homicide* and worked as a producer and director on other series including *The Sullivans*, *The Flying Doctors*, *Cop Shop* and *Prisoner*. In recent years he has been featured in numerous Australian films including *Wog Boy*, *Breaker Morant*, *The Craic*, *The Castle*, *The Dish*, *Innocence* and

Human Touch. In 2004 Pan Macmillan published his autobiography (written with Peter Wilmoth), *Bud, A Life*.

My memory banks seem to take me back to my early
years in Coogee in Sydney. I believe I was christened
in the St Nicholas Church – the Church of England
as it was in those days. I think my parents were
married there and my mother was a great friend of
the daughter of the vicar, Mr Greenwood. It seemed
natural that as soon as I was old enough I went to
Sunday School. I can still remember being intrigued
by stories about Christ. I can clearly remember
thinking what a great person he would be to know;
not in the standard religious sense, but as a person. I
had a strong feeling that he must have been a good
bloke to talk to.

When I was about fourteen or fifteen I became a
Sunday School teacher. Very junior, of course. My
youngest brother, Pat, came into my class. He was
born on St Patrick's Day so had an immediate nickname despite the fact that he was to have been
christened Harvey Bryce. That was the plan. The vicar
got it a little wrong and said, 'I christen thee Patrick
Harvey Bryce', so the nickname became official.

The fact that my brother was in my class was my
undoing. Entering the difficult teenage years meant
I was somewhat less than calm at home. I remember
having arguments with Mum or Dad or both and
being, I am sure, completely unreasonable, and then
having to face my little brother in the Sunday School
class as if nothing had happened. The hypocrisy was

a bit difficult to live with, so I managed to get out of my Sunday duties.

I was soon to qualify as a junior in the Coogee Surf Club and Sunday patrols took over. But somehow I never lost that strong feeling that Christ must have been a 'beaut bloke'. What he was reported to have said made sense. Europe was surging towards yet another war and hatred seemed to be bubbling up everywhere. Refugees were starting to arrive in Australia and nice neighbours of German origin were feeling uncomfortable.

The reasonable advice given on The Mount seemed not to have been remembered or even thought about. Why *not* try forgiveness, rather than revenge? Why *not* turn the other cheek instead of building more powerful aircraft and bigger tanks and guns? It was worth a try. We had time. Not much, but a little. But soon the war was upon us. I learned to fly aeroplanes in the RAAF and somehow survived the war.

Many of us innocently believed that there would be no more wars after the horrendous bombing campaigns, with bigger and bigger bombs, conventional and atomic. But soon there was Korea and skirmishes everywhere becoming real wars all over again. And it seemed the advice offered 2000 years ago was yet to be really tried.

But there was at last a glow of hope on the horizon. After twenty-seven years in gaol, Nelson Mandela came back on the scene. Revenge could have been forgiven. But it did not happen. Instead, at last, forgiveness was in the air and a new version of South Africa was born. There must have been difficulties everywhere, but somehow there was a new and peaceful nation where there had seemed no hope. I believe we should look to what has happened there and think about it. It could be the clue that we have been needing and the glimmer of hope that might save this extraordinary world.

Nicholas Tonti-Fillipini

Dr Nicholas Tonti-Filippini BA (Hons), MA (Monash), PhD (Melb) is a consultant ethicist and lectures in medical ethics. He has suffered from renal disease for thirty years and been dependent on haemodialysis (4 x 4 hour sessions per week) for the past twelve years. He is married to Dr Mary Walsh, a medical practitioner, and they have four children aged 10–18.

The Prodigal Generation

> Now, this bell tolling softly for another, says to me: Thou must die.
>
> John Donne

I am a baby-boomer, more privileged, more educated (three university degrees for which I paid no fees), and more selfish than any generation before or since. But we are now ageing and feeling the vulnerability of declining ability, health and fitness, and relegation to the retiring or soon to be retired.

What we baby boomers fear most is that we shall reap as we have sown. We have expounded the doctrine of autonomy and self-actualisation. We deserted our own parents in nursing homes, and now we face the prospect of relying on the doubtful generosity of our children's generation whom we neglected through failed marriages and the many other consequences of our own drive for individualism and personal freedom. As a result of our own self-indulgence, there are also so very few of them to bear the burden of our ageing.

The bell that tolls for us tolls, not with a melancholy ring calling to human hearts, but the ugly, cracked and empty sound of a community sundered by self-interest: toneless, dull.

This is our vulnerability. We denied ourselves a venerable old age, sentencing ourselves to neglect. As we lived so we also plan to die, at our own hands, at a time and place of our own choosing, individuals to the last, lonely, angry, resenting the reality that we created, unable to accept the powerlessness of ageing and unwilling to continue when control passes to others, as it must.

We represent the failure of Individualism, the crushing reality that because we have lived as we have lived, in our old age and in our deaths we are nothing. It was this thought that made me turn to John Donne:

> No man is an Iland, intire of itselfe;
> . . . any man's death diminishes me, because I am
> involved in Mankinde;
> And therefore never send to know for whom
> the bell tolls;
> It tolls for thee.

The particular vulnerability of our ageing developed in the choice of indulgence over love, Individualism over Communitarianism. Our glorious impieties are reduced to a tragedy, a revolt against the inevitable.

If there is a message that we can give to the X, Y and dotcom generations, it is to learn from our excesses. The self-actualisation we sought was a kind of madness. We looked for love, we looked for experience, we depended on science for our satisfaction and our triumph over the human condition, but we neglected a central element of self-knowledge: self-fulfilment and expression of personality happen in outreach to others not within ourselves. We looked inwards not outwards. We wanted love but were least willing to give it unconditionally.

We formed relationships of convenience and dropped them when they became inconvenient. The few who had children adopted rules of manu-facture and quality control. Our parenting is done by others, scientific and by remote control, quality time rather than love. We embraced unquestioningly the eugenics that science gave us in the form of genetic diagnosis and selective abortion. We embraced repro-ductive technology to overcome the infertility which we had, mostly, created, either through waiting too long to realise other priorities or by damaging it through medical suppression, or by disease resulting from our promiscuity.

True happiness is won by willingness to suffer, to subvert hedonism for something larger than self. Love and suffering are a partnership: the more we love the greater the potential for suffering, but that suffering has meaning and purpose because it is for love. Love is the response to suffering and the occasion for the building of friendships. We are the great indebted. We failed ourselves. We failed to be community builders either at home or outside it. We were the prodigal generation. We were not lovers.

LUCY TURNBULL

Lucy Hughes Turnbull has lived in Sydney all her life. She has worked as a solicitor and investment banker, and in 1999 published a book called *Sydney – Biography of a City*.

Lucy was Lord Mayor (2003–4) and Deputy Lord Mayor (1999–2003) of the City of Sydney Council, the first woman to hold both positions.

Lucy is now devoting her time to her business and not-for-profit interests. She is the Chair of FTR Holdings Limited, a technology company listed on the Australian Stock Exchange. She sits on the board of several other companies. She is a director of the Sydney Cancer Foundation and a member of the board of the Museum of Contemporary Art. She and her husband established the Turnbull Foundation, a charitable trust. Lucy's interests are history, politics, architecture, and contemporary culture.

The Christian Bible tells us that the most important thing of all is love. Love of God, love of all others, and the injunction to live a life full of love. This multi-faceted idea of love is hard enough to understand, let alone follow. This kind of love cannot be the same love as we feel for our friends and family, because love of the unknown – God and everyone on earth – quite a different thing. Much more abstract and much more complex and demanding.

The meaning of the words in the Bible cannot be 'love' in a familiar sense. So what does this Christian 'love' mean? The only sense in which I can understand it is if you interpret 'love' as meaning that we should always act with good intentions, and strive to never have hate in our hearts. We must not rush to act when provoked. We cannot counter hate with hate, evil with evil.

Hate and anger are the most destructive emotions in the world today, just as they always have been. They fuel and create evil and cause conflict because they make it possible for one group or tribe to dehumanise another.

I believe that every human being should strive to understand those who stand on the other side of the fence, whether that fence is political, racial or social, whether the people on the other side of the 'fence' live down the road, across the barricades in a war zone or on the other side of the world oceans away.

At the same time, we must understand, and teach our children to understand the difference between right and wrong, good and evil, without developing the idea that 'wrong' or 'evil' is limited to any particular group of people or their beliefs. And we must teach them, by example above all else, that living a life motivated by hate and anger is wrong.

If parents and other people important in children's lives – teachers, community and political leaders, teach the young by their words and their example, to hate and to dehumanise others, the moral framework is set for future generations.

We must always look for the goodness in others and strive to live a life free of hatred and anger. That can be difficult, indeed it is one of the hardest tests for any human being, but it is also the ultimate test of our humanity. To believe or to act otherwise is to make it possible to slide from living in a civilised society into a world of brutality. When that happens, any act of violence or abuse can be justified.

Twenty or thirty years ago we thought that hatred and the dehumanisation of others was isolated to horrible periods in history, such as in Nazi Germany and during the Stalinist era in the Soviet Union, and during the regime of Pol Pot in Cambodia. We thought such a disintegration of human values was inconceivable in the present day, in so many places around the world. Even fifteen years ago, there was such hope and optimism about the future of world peace when the East–West political divide fell away in 1989 with the collapse of communism.

But sadly, we now know that our optimistic hopes for the future have not come true. We know that hatred and cruelty are as prevalent as they ever were, and that they are still the cause of almost inconceivable violence and loss of life – such as the extermination of 800,000 people through civil war in Rwanda in 1994, in Sudan today, and other wars around the world, and in recent years in conflicts and terrorist attacks in the Middle East and Israel, in the USA and on our own back door in Bali.

We can be stunned and in a state of disbelief about

the consequences of hatred. But how do we do something about it?

It is a big journey, but it must begin with a few simple steps, and the first of these is to make parents, teachers and community leaders understand that cycle of hatred and anger must stop and that this will only stop if they teach their children that hatred is self defeating, and that nothing good will ever come of it.

TERRY UNDERWOOD

Terry Underwood juggles the roles of wife, mother, cattle-woman, nurse, bookkeeper, cook, gardener, photographer and counsellor each day on her remote Riveren Station, 600 kilometres south-west of Katherine in the Northern Territory. Her overnight best-selling autobiography *In The Middle Of Nowhere,* an Australian classic, is currently in its fourteenth edition. Terry's photographic sequel *Riveren: My Home, Our Country* is also much loved. A tireless and passionate ambassador for the bush and its people, Terry is a highly sought-after speaker. The Katherine Icon, her magnificent project for 2002 – Australia's Year of the Outback – is a lasting tribute to the pastoral industry's pioneers.

My personal creed was infused within my soul at the moment of my conception.

My childhood was steeped in traditional Catholic practices. Beside my family at Mass I recited the Nicene Creed: 'I believe in one God, the Father Almighty, maker of heaven and earth . . .'

Yet religion extended beyond the church. The dogmas of faith, hope and charity were applied to our daily lives and the purpose of our existence. Mum and Dad reminded their children often that more things are wrought by prayer than this world dreams of and the family that prays together stays together.

Within our home of security and love, devoted parents nurtured us. Beyond our front gate, a world of excitement and relative predictability beckoned.

Throughout adolescence I tried to uphold those instilled values and principles. I knew the difference between right and wrong and there were home grown signposts and standards. There were rules. It was important to please rather than to hurt or disappoint.

Following my man to the back of beyond as a new bride in the 1960s proved my unshakeable belief in the power of love. He, the experienced visionary cattleman, and I, the city nurse, stood together to face the challenges that were relentlessly thrust upon us. To build our own cattle station from scratch a long, long way from the rest of the world was incredibly demanding and ultimately fulfilling.

My adulthood has transpired in God's own cathedral – the Outback of Australia. Here the splendour and intricacies of His creation are inescapable. This timeless land is stunningly beautiful, but also treacherous and unforgiving. He is our Keeper.

Living each moment so fully, I am spiritually connected to this place, its people and the creatures I love so passionately. We are all intertwined, dependent yet independent, but always made vulnerable by our mortality.

As a convert from the city, I discovered that those who work the land must become of that land in order to survive. Today we have a growing population dependent upon, but perhaps less appreciative of, the vital food chain. The country-city divide must be reduced by the exchange of stories and experiences on a broad scale.

On September 11, 2001 the universe changed for everyone. Our Prime Minister, Mrs Howard and their son were profoundly affected by the terrorists' attack, a cancer of a hideous dimension, because they were in the United States at the time. But in effect we were all there – unable to comprehend, crying with broken hearts because humankind had been betrayed by its own. The cancer continues to spread insidiously.

Tough times multiply for us all, irrespective of who we are or where we live. In this unforeseen era of fear, tragedy and uncertainty, it is up to each of us to focus and lead, to help and heal, and to love. There can never be too much love

Jason McCartney's account of Bali made me weep. As a human fireball, his concerns were solely for his missing mates. If only this were a worldwide trait.

What has happened to commitment, accountability and compassion? There is too much preoccupation with individual rights instead of responsibilities.

As I write this the bereaved people of Madrid grieve the loss of beloved family and friends brutally killed and maimed by terrorists. The Spanish have rallied in their anguish and outrage against the forces of evil. They too believe that the spirit of humanity cannot be extinguished.

The strength of our communities lies in the strength of our families, and the strength of our families lies in love. Love for each other, and for the land we live in, and which lives in us.

Cao Van Nguyen

Fr Cao Van Nguyen SJ, a refugee from Vietnam, came to Australia at the end of 1982. He grew up during the Vietnam War and the persecution under the hands of the new regime after 1975. Leaving behind his own family, he escaped by boat with 158 others, arrived on Malaysian shores, and was then placed in the Pulau Bidong refugee camp.

He joined the Jesuits in 1986 and after thirteen years of training he graduated as a Bachelor of Theology, a Bachelor of Art and a Master of Theological Studies in Melbourne. He was ordained as a Jesuit priest in the Catholic Church in 1998. He was appointed director of Jesuit Refugee Service Australia in 2000.

Amen. This I believe.

Compassion and generosity. Everyone is capable of both. Compassion and generosity can be instant, or built-in – the culmination of a learning process. Although it is in each person, it can be contaminated by greed, selfishness, fear, worry, prestige, personal perceptions, opinion, political parties and the like. I remember that when I was living in Pulau Bidong refugee camp in Malaysia as a boat person I heard from many people about how compassionate and generous Australians were. Because of this, I was accepted and resettled in Australia. However, I have wondered about the generosity of Australians since 2000 when I began my work as Co-ordinator of Jesuit Refugee Service Australia.

I still believe that Australians are always generous to the poor and the needy, especially refugees and asylum seekers who are the poorest of the poor. However, Australians' compassion and generosity might be contaminated in some ways. A political party's policy? Fear? Racism? I do not think that racism is the main reason, but fear is.

Over twenty-one years of living in Australia I have had many opportunities to ask people about reasons for racism but there has never been a satisfactory answer. I could sense the fear they projected. Fear of being overcrowded with Asians. Fear of unemployment: they blame Asian refugees and migrants who came to take over jobs. The image of 'Us' and 'Them' was greatly embedded in their minds. Fear of invasion by refugees. This is why a few Middle Eastern asylum seekers who arrived legally by boat were detained, while the thousands of illegal European visa over-stayers live freely in the community.

Since 2000, fear of invasion is not only personal any more. It has become national and public. Border control policy has contaminated the generosity and compassion of Australians as a whole. The fear of terrorism has been exploited and has infected every Australian regardless of our backgrounds or whether I am an Iraqi, Afghan, Vietnamese, Chinese, Sudanese, Ethiopian or any other former nationality. This fear is repeatedly reinforced in our minds. I believe that as a result we, Australians, have become more and more hostile to refugees and asylum seekers.

The movement of people from one place to another has occurred since the beginning of the world. The oldest source is the Bible which described the movement of Israelites from one nation to another, escaping persecution and hardship. Why should we limit and prevent the movement of people?

Imagine the water in a river peacefully flowing. If it is blocked it cannot bring life to the land it reached before. The river is under pressure where it is blocked, until one day it holds no longer and breaks every obstacle, and causes much damage, to maintain its flow.

I believe that in any situation a person tries to bring the best out of the worst. In the worst situation of all – faced with life or death – a person has no choice. They will choose life even if there is only the tiniest chance of survival. I remember that when I decided to escape across the sea to a refugee camp I was conscious that there was the smallest chance for me to live. In that case I had no choice but to go ahead with the hope that at least there would be a chance to live in a free country. I accepted the narrow door of life. Death for me at that time was just my fate. In religious language, it was God's providence or plan. If God wanted me to live and had plans for me I would be alive. If God called me in the journey I would be happy to leave this life. A refugee or an asylum seeker is in a similar situation – accepting the worst and trying to bring the best out of it.

Sometimes, the best is not good enough. The results could be less than one hopes for. The results could be failure. Instinctively, one can become despairing if the failure is reinforced and one is blamed. The last thing one needs is blame when one fails. What one really needs is not blame but someone to understand, to believe in, to encourage and to challenge, so as to help one stand firm.

I believe in hope. Hope brings direction to the future. Hope encourages people to face challenges – even the worst. Hope brings courage and life. Hope reassures people to go forward even if there is little chance to succeed.

MARK WAHLQVIST

Professor Mark Wahlqvist, AO, B Med Sc, MD, BS (Adelaide), MD (Uppsala), FRACP, FAIFST, FAFPHM, FACN, FTSE, is a physician and nutritionist. He has held Chairs in Human Nutrition, Food Sciences, Medicine, Health and Behavioural Sciences at various universities over some twenty-seven years. He has published twenty or more books and about 500 scientific papers in the biomedical sciences, food and nutrition sciences, and in public health. Currently he is Chair of the National Nutrition Committee of the Australian Academy of Sciences, Editor-in-Chief of the *Asia Pacific Journal of Clinical Nutrition*, and of www.healthyeatingclub.org, and President of the International Union of Nutritional Sciences, a member Union of the International Council for Science. His wife, Dr Huang Soo Sien, whom he met at Adelaide Medical School, and with whom he has two children, Dr Ingmar Wei Tzu Wahlqvist and Kerstin Yih Fen Wahlqvist, died in April 2004.

Belief is characteristic of humans. It reflects knowledge, experience and connection to things living and inanimate, past, present and future, and earthly and cosmological. It is the 'connectedness' of belief which gives it a spiritual quality. It is 'belief about' rather than 'belief in' which is the more robust and sustainable concept. This is why belief at its best is more spiritual than religious.

In 2003, my soul-mate and spouse, Huang Soo Sien, suffered a devastating haemorrhagic stroke and could scarcely speak to me, although, with great comprehension and skill on her part, she communicated wonderfully. Now I understand that the belief about which I have previously written has been ours together. Her stroke was not explicable with contemporary medical knowledge or risk analysis, except that it was very unlikely on the basis of studies of Europeans. But she is Chinese and we, medical practitioners by training, who met as fellow students, have endeavoured to integrate the different perspectives of orient and occident that inform our lives, our science, and our professional practice. Understandably, we did not fully achieve this. We both believed this pursuit must continue for future generations, especially if we are to reduce the risk of tragedies like that which beset Soo.

And what do we now believe about that for which we have struggled, worked and lived? Soo is sorely missed at home, work and play, but her generosity, sense of joy about simple things, belief in others, and efforts to change our fortunes for the better will live and grow for generations amongst her immediate and extended family, her friends and patients. The world is a better place because of Soo's beliefs about people, the respect due to them and their potential; about nature, the respect due to it and the pleasure it provides; about music and song, its ability to harmonise and lift the spirits; and about the cosmos, thinking with universality of mind and providing for forces which we are yet to comprehend. We met and fell in love in 1960 amidst racism, intolerance, duplicity and prejudice, all of which we believed were unacceptable. But finally Soo was surrounded by the love and care of both religious and irreligious people, people of various belief systems, Buddhist, Jewish, Muslim, Christian and Animist. We have come a long way with the fabric of our beliefs, but we must remain vigilant unless even this be unpicked and trampled.

While, by its nature, the future is uncertain, beliefs which are constructive and contributory, creative and visionary, ones of dependability and loyalty, diligence and perseverance (without being perseverant), which are rational and integrative, and at all times tolerant of all but intolerance, can make it a future most hopeful and peaceful.

KERRY WALKER

Kerry Walker is an actor who graduated from NIDA in 1974. Since then, she has divided her theatre work between new Australian writing and the classics. She has appeared in numerous film, television and radio productions. In 1994 she was awarded an AM for Services to the Performing Arts.

When I read John's letter asking me for a personal statement of belief, my immediate response was to write about why I believe Australia needs a Bill of Rights. I believe that our current system of government no longer offers its citizens adequate protection. I sense a whittling away of decency – it's hard to think of Australia today as the land of the 'fair go' without a sour kind of irony. Those great binding sentiments of ours – our healthy scepticism, our sense of justice and common kindness – are receding into a sepia twilight.

Under the rule of the Howard government, I believe that Australia is greatly diminished. And that more than ever we need a unifying statement of beliefs: a standard against which to measure the weasel words and shabby actions of those who seek to re-make Australia in their own image.

There are many examples of the way our country is becoming 'atomised'; broken into little groups of competing self-interest. The one that comes first to mind right now is our rulers' treatment of refugees. The cynical exploitation of frightened families for political advantage is simply inhumane. It weakens the things we thought made us strong.

Yet I passionately believe that the majority of Australians have not had their consciences excised. The generous national response year after year to the annual bushfire horrors proves that.

So – why the gap?

I believe that it is a fundamental lack of imagination on the part of our rulers. This inability or refusal to empathise – to put themselves in the shoes of those less fortunate – is their fatal flaw – and it leads them to think that only fear tactics will get them re-elected. Not only does this result in the de-humanising of people fleeing war, violence and oppression – but it weakens us all.

It's a short step from despair to defeatism – but it's a step we don't have to take.

A Bill of Rights won't put food on anyone's table; it won't pull down a single metre of razor wire. But it might just help remind us of the better things about Australia – it might help give us all a sense of belonging, a stronger sense that the Aboriginal woman struggling to keep her family together in Townsville breathes the same oxygen as that bloke who's just been laid off in Launceston. It might help clear away the moral fogginess generated by the current administration and its more pungent media cheer-leaders.

For those who put their faith in each other rather than the supernatural, W.H. Auden's 'We must love one another or die' is all that's needed. But it's a statement that could easily have come from Christ or Mohammed.

Idealistic? I can't think of a time when we've needed ideals more. As the international situation becomes more complex, the natural reaction of governments is to want more powers to control their citizens – the argument being that national security requires the surrender of some personal liberties. This is where the needs of a government (coupled with a desire to maintain power) and the needs of citizens can diverge.

Here, a Bill of Rights can act as a counter-balance – a guarantee that whatever the circumstances, the rights of Australians remain sovereign – the people saying: this far and no further.

True, elections can change governments, but one thing is certain: rights taken away are rarely given back.

The process of getting a Bill of Rights will have to start with education in schools, and it will need to evolve as a specifically Australian document, conscious of our history and the uniqueness of our people. It can't happen quickly – it may take years – but the conversation needs to begin.

ARCHIE WELLER

Archie Weller is a short-story writer, novelist, playwright, poet and lecturer. He was born in Subiaco, Western Australia in 1957. At a young age Archie was encouraged to write by his mother, and by Jack Davis, who published some of his stories in the magazine *Aboriginal Identity*. Archie worked at a variety of different jobs, including as a wharf labourer and a medical orderly. He was gaoled in Broome for three months, after which he wrote *The Day of the Dog*, his first full length novel. Published by Allen & Unwin, Archie's novel was the runner-up in the inaugural Vogel Award. With Paul Radley's confession in 1996 that he had not in fact written the winning entry, *Jack Rivers and Me*, Archie considers he became, by default, the inaugural winner.

In 1991, *Day of the Dog* was made into the film *Black-fellas*, which won several AFI awards. Archie's second book, *Going Home*, a collection of short stories, was published by Allen & Unwin in 1986, and his third, the novel *The Land of the Golden Clouds*, was published in 1998, also by Allen & Unwin. It won the Human Rights Award for that year, presented by the Governor-General.

Archie's fourth book is an historical novel about the effects of white settlement on Aborigines in south Western Australia. He is currently working on a long essay on the plight of the white-skinned Aboriginal, in which he deplores the increasing tendency to denigrate people, including himself, who claim

Aboriginality but who are not obviously full-bloods. As Archie says, the percentage of Aboriginal blood is not important; what is important is how much pride an individual takes in that percentage.

When I was three years old my grandmother died, up in Perth. At the same time I woke up, crying in great distress. When I was about seven I almost drowned in the water hole on the family farm – a farm said to have been cursed by the local Nyoongahs because of a murder committed there. All those years later it was the white shadowy figure of a man I saw which lured me down into the cold dark depths. When I was seventeen my other grandmother died. I went to collect my mother's handbag and heard footsteps in the corridor, and saw the lips of my grandmother's portrait move. Her face came alive and she seemed to be telling me something. At that stage I was too afraid to wait around and see what she was saying. To this day I regret not accepting what would have been a glorious meeting with a much-loved old woman.

Throughout my life I have had many experiences of a spiritual nature; feelings for a place or person as to whether they were good or bad. On my sister's horse stud I saw shadows running while I heard screaming and horses galloping. It was not until much later I learned about a massacre of the local people who were, incidentally, innocent of the crime they were accused of. Over east I can sense the joy or sadness of many places and it has been a habit of mine to quietly ask the spirits there permission for me to pass.

What I truly believe in is the spirit world. But not the New Age spirit world, with its gurus and mantras, crystals and tarot cards, dream-catchers and astrology charts, tea leaves, witches and mystic gypsies, although there is some of that I believe in. The spirit world I am interested in is as old as the human world and as inexplicable as the Sidhe of the Irish. I would call the Sidhe another name for the spirits that frequent my world. Perhaps I would call them the 'greys' that those among us who believe in aliens would say are visitors from another planet. I would also call those spirits the angels and demons from the Bible.

Recently I met a beautiful, very spiritual Christian woman. At last I am studying the much translated, much read Bible. The incredibly complex letter and number system to be found, for example, in the beginning of Genesis or the beginning of St Matthew's Gospel utterly amazes me, no less than the possibility of other life-forms being out in space. GOD – such a small word yet so complex a character. Do I believe in Him? I don't consider Him a male. God is the biggest spirit in the universe. I believe God is many-faceted, each of us having a unique individual mind, and if God created us in His image then God, too, has a mind – the most brilliant mind of all.

I believe in LIFE: L for Love, I for Intellectual Interests and Imagination, F for Friendship, Fun and

Frolics, E for Excitement. Every morning begins a new life for me and in each day I strive to find three beautiful, unusual things: a song bird, a butterfly, a smile on a stranger's face, the look in the eyes of my lover, a dog chasing its tail, a child on a swing, a phrase in a poem or book. I devour each day with a fierce intensity.

In bed at night the dreams come. Dreams play a huge part in my psyche. They always have and always will. When I close my eyes I wonder which dream – or nightmare – will visit me this night. I think it is a part of the spirit world I so embrace and one day will enter . . . I hope.

Maureen Wheeler

At the age of twenty Maureen Wheeler left Belfast, Northern Ireland to travel the world. Three days later she met Tony Wheeler on a park bench in London and one year later they married and drove overland to Afghanistan. By various means they continued to Australia, arriving just as Gough Whitlam became Prime Minister. Together they founded Lonely Planet, travelled the world, had two children and somehow managed to stay married. Maureen was named by the Business Women's Network as the 'Most Inspiring Businesswoman in Australia' and was made an honorary Doctor of Letters by the University of Ulster.

I grew up in Belfast, which is the main city of Northern Ireland, part of the United Kingdom. When I was a teenager the IRA began a campaign of terror to unify Ireland. The problem was that many people in Northern Ireland didn't want to be a part of Ireland, but instead wanted to remain British.

Belfast is a small city, smaller than Adelaide. I had three girlfriends, Mary, Eileen and Jennifer. I was not a Catholic, but my three friends were. We went everywhere together. We would meet in town and go ice skating, or to discos, or to Blues clubs to hear live music or we would go to one of the many bars where you could listen and sing along to Irish music, played by old men with cloth caps and long coats. Until the 'troubles' started I had always felt safe in Belfast. We would walk home late at night when I had missed the last bus; we couldn't afford taxis. We would stop and buy fish and chips and talk about our plans to leave Ireland and see the world.

When the troubles started the soldiers were billeted in the ice rink, we were searched going into buildings, and armoured cars and soldiers with machine guns patrolled the streets. Whole streets disappeared overnight and buses and cars were commandeered to barricade neighbourhoods against the police, the army, each other.

I learned that when you read the headlines 'ten people injured' and feel relief that they didn't die, the word 'wounded' can hide the fact that those people may now have to live with the most horrendous injuries, which change their lives for ever.

Mary, Jennifer, Eileen and I kept going out, kept trying to lead a 'normal' life. The heightened tension did not affect our friendship. Even when I left for London, we partied late the night before and promised to keep in touch.

Some months later Eileen called me to say that I was not to open the newspaper. Jennifer and her sister had been out to choose a wedding and bridesmaid's dress for her sister's wedding. They had stopped at our favourite café for a coffee, a place where we had met every Saturday afternoon for years. A bomb was under their table. Jennifer lost both legs, her sister lost a leg, an arm and an eye.

My friends came out to Australia for my fiftieth birthday and although we had a wonderful time I realised how, for Jennifer, life has to be negotiated every single day, and how even simple things can become an exhausting, frustrating process and no matter how courageous you are, you never really get used to it.

The troubles lasted a long time in Ireland. Now all those 'hard men' who spoke of their ideals and their justifications have largely moved on. Some went to prison, some still try to rouse others to continue the fight, some are politicians.

If there is one thing I now believe it is that terrorism is just that – the spreading of terror, pain and suffering. Whatever the justification, whatever the 'cause', no one has the right to claim their 'cause' justifies killing or maiming innocent people. A cause will always have several 'sides' but people only get one chance at life and no one has the right to take that away in order to make a point. Sure there are injustices in the world, and there is unwarranted suffering, but to be prepared to kill people for a particular cause is to create more injustice and more suffering that spreads out way beyond the cause itself. No one has the right to decide that some people are expendable, in order that their own beliefs should prevail.

TONY WHEELER

In the early seventies Tony and Maureen Wheeler left London in an elderly Mini, intending to drive as far east as British automotive engineering would carry them. It carried them all the way to Afghanistan. Months later they landed from a New Zealand yacht on Western Australia's North-West Cape and hitch-hiked across to Sydney, arriving with 27 cents between them. The book they wrote about their Asian adventures became the very first Lonely Planet guidebook. Today Lonely Planet has over 600 different titles and Tony has written or contributed substantially to more than thirty of them.

'Where are you from?' we asked.

They'd been puzzling us from the moment they arrived at the boat jetty. We were catching a *vaporetto*, the Venetian 'bus service', back to the Venice train station to get the last train of the evening to Verona. Just before the boat pulled in a noisy group of tourists crowded into the 'bus' shelter. Where were they from? We couldn't identify their language but their slightly out-of-date looking clothes indicated they might have been from one of the less successful old Eastern European nations. Bulgaria perhaps?

The *vaporetto* pulled in, we set off along the canal towards the station and with my friends we went out to the open section at the stern. A few minutes later a young man detached himself from the mysterious group and joined us. He identified himself as the tour group leader and spent ten minutes joking about the drawbacks of his occupation: two exhausting weeks trying to cover all of Italy, the guy who always got lost, the homesick women who couldn't wait to get home, the couple who simply weren't happy with unfamiliar Italian food.

'But where are you from?' we finally asked. 'We've been trying to guess which country.'

'Palestine,' he replied.

Just ordinary tourists, out to see the world, just like us.

I believe that travel really is important. Oh sure, it's enjoyable, that's the main reason we travel. And more people are employed in travel and tourism than any other field of business, so for many people it's what puts bread on the table. Yet travel is far more than fun and dollars, it's how we meet the outside world. That chance encounter with Palestine in Italy was a reminder that it's travel which turns people from one-dimensional stereotypes, conjured up by media and politicians, into real human beings.

Travel to Turkey and you'll quickly discover that most Turks are unbelievably hospitable and kindhearted. The image they've been saddled with by films like *Midnight Express* is simply not true. It's the same anywhere and it's only by going there that you come face to face with that reality. I love looking out of aeroplane windows, watching the world unfold beneath me, but I'm always aware of the unbelievable separation between me, sipping my wine, and the real world below. From cruising altitude planet earth always looks beautiful. There's no sign of poverty, famine or war, all of which might be just 10 km away.

I'm convinced that if George W. Bush had just a little more curiosity about the world outside Texas when he was younger the world might be a better place today. How did somebody who resolutely avoided going anywhere outside the US come to be the leader of the free world? Perhaps if he had just travelled a little he would have been less convinced that everything can be solved with smart technology launched from 10,000 metres above ground level.

Get down to ground level and the view changes. Seeing the world in close up might be painful but more often it's a reminder that at the end of the day we're looking for the same things – security, comfort, a better future for our kids, a better world for all of us. All the TV, movies, magazines and web-sites in the world are nothing more than varied versions of virtual reality. None of them is more than a looking glass into the real world. It's only by travel that we find it.

DAVID WILLIAMSON

David Williamson's first full-length play, *The Coming of Stork,* premiered at the La Mama Theatre, Carlton, in 1970 and later became the film *Stork,* directed by Tim Burstall. *The Removalists* and *Don's Party* followed in 1971, then *Jugglers Three* (1972), *What If You Died Tomorrow?* (1973), *The Department* (1975), *A Handful of Friends* (1976), *The Club* (1977) and *Travelling North* (1979). In 1972 *The Removalists* won the Australian Writers' Guild AWGIE Award for best stage play and the best script in any medium and the British production saw Williamson nominated as Most Promising Playwright by the London *Evening Standard.*

The 1980s saw his success continue with *Celluloid Heroes* (1980), *The Perfectionist* (1982), *Sons of Cain* (1985), *Emerald City* (1987) and *Top Silk* (1989); whilst the 1990s produced *Siren* (1990), *Money and Friends* (1991), *Brilliant Lies* (1993), *Sanctuary* (1994), *Dead White Males* (1995), *Heretic* (1996), *Third World Blues* (an adaptation of *Jugglers Three)* and *After the Ball* (both in 1997), and *Corporate Vibes* and *Face to Face* (both in 1999). *The Great Man* (2000), *Up for Grabs, A Conversation, Charitable Intent* (all in 2001), *Soulmates* (2002), *Birthrights* (2003), *Amigos* and *Flatfoot* (both in 2004) have since followed.

Williamson is widely recognised as Australia's most successful playwright and over the last thirty years his plays have been performed throughout Australia and produced in Britain, the United States, Canada and many European countries. A number of his stage works have been adapted for the screen, including *The Removalists*, *Don's Party*, *The Club*, *Travelling North*, *Emerald City*, *Sanctuary* and *Brilliant Lies.*

David Williamson has won the Australian Film Institute film script award for *Petersen* (1974), *Don's Party* (1976), *Gallipoli* (1981) and *Travelling North* (1987) and has won eleven Australian Writers' Guild AWGIE Awards. He lives on Queensland's Sunshine Coast with his writer wife, Kristin Williamson.

When you read many self improvement tracts and messages of advice about how to lead one's life, you often hear the advice that you should try and spend your life doing what you intrinsically love. This sort of advice tells you to 'listen for your song' and when you've heard it to follow that instinct and go flat out trying to live your life in tune with it.

The theory of course is that it's far better to be earning your living doing something you love than wasting eight hours a day on a drudgery you hate in order to finance the rest of your life, in which you do things that really matter. This was something my own father stressed. He spent his life working in a bank and told me late in life that he hated every day. The routine boredom and endless attention to detail didn't appeal to him. He urged me to find the direction in life I wanted to go and to follow it.

While it's plainly true that to spend one's life earning money by doing something you hate is not a recipe for happiness, I sometimes feel that the thought that there is only one true path in life can bring agonies of its own.

I always secretly wanted to be a writer, but I didn't know what sort of writer until some time in my twenties. The magic of the interaction between actor and audience attracted me strongly to drama. And I did try hard to become a playwright and luckily I was in the right place at the right time with the right type of talent.

But in the meantime I had done an engineering degree and taught fluid mechanics and thermo-dynamics at the Swinburne Institute of Technology while I studied psychology at Melbourne Univer-sity. I'd started a post graduate course in psychology when my playwrighting career took off and I have been able to spend the rest of my life, to date, doing what I'd always wanted. I was lucky.

But the interesting thing, looking back, is that I was perfectly happy teaching at Swinburne, with a friendly staff and good students. I enjoyed teach-ing. It involved human interaction, humour and the satisfaction of teaching students something that would help them find a career. I had no deep passion for engineering, but I felt I was doing something worthwhile. On planes I still occasionally meet someone who thrusts a business card at me and tells me that I taught them thermodynamics.

I also enjoyed psychology. The same obsessive interest in personality and temperament that led me into playwrighting fuelled my interest in psychology. If the playwrighting had not taken over

I'm sure I would've ended up a research academic in psychology and been perfectly happy.

I guess what I'm trying to say is that the view that there is one true path in life is an oversimplification. There are probably many paths which are capable of making us feel fulfilled. I've met very sad and bitter people who have been convinced that all they ever wanted was, for instance, to be a playwright, and when it hasn't happened for them, they felt their life was somehow a failure.

From my perspective, after all these years, playwrighting is another form of work. Hard work. It has the downside of being solitary work so that I miss those days of easy camaraderie with my students and fellow staff. It's also an exposed line of work. Everyone feels entitled to tell you exactly what they think of your work. It's work which has high levels of anxiety. You worry whether your latest play will succeed or not with critics and audiences. The upside is that when it does work there's a great feeling, as an audience patently finds meaning in what you've done.

Every life path has its credits and debits and it's highly likely that most of us could make a great success of many more than one life path.

And finally it's one's loved ones, one's family and friends, who bring the highest levels of satisfaction to life. My belief is that there's not one song out there, but many. Don't obsess about what might have been. Enjoy what is.

PAUL WILSON

Paul Wilson is the author or co-author of twenty-eight books on crime and social issues including *Jean Lee: The Last Woman Hanged in Australia* and *Murder in Tandem: When Two People Kill*. He was a regular columnist for six years for Brisbane's *Courier Mail* and before that for six years with the *Herald Sun* in Melbourne. He has been Dean of Humanities and Social Sciences at two Australian Universities and is currently Chair of Criminology at Bond University on the Gold Coast. In 2003 Professor Wilson was awarded the Order of Australia medal for his contributions to criminology and education. He is currently finishing his first novel with the intriguing title of *White Trash*, which is a thriller set in Asia and Australia.

Like thousands of other Australians I have been the victim of crime. My house has been broken into, I once was the victim of a massive property fraud and I have also been physically assaulted. Like most other victims I wanted the offenders to be punished and thoughts of revenge and imprisonment were at the forefront of my mind.

Yet personal emotions are not necessarily instructive signposts for useful social policy. I doubt that the feelings of retribution which consume most victims of crime help very much when it comes to implementing programs and policies to prevent crime.

Despite my own experience as a victim I have always firmly believed that the amount of crime we have in our country depends largely on social factors. The greater the gap between the haves and have-nots, the more unemployment and the more we value consumption – especially conspicuous consumption – the more crime and violence we will have.

The growth of a neo-conservative philosophy that views social welfare and human rights as a matter of personal responsibility rather than a concern for government reinforces the view that individuals, and not social forces and policies, are responsible for crime. Accordingly, the criminal justice system, and especially imprisonment, is seen as the basic solution to crime and, for that matter, most of our other social problems like drugs and excessive alcohol consumption.

Now I do not deny that people who commit crime have to take responsibility for their actions and that some sort of punishment is usually necessary for those who steal property and commit acts of violence. But I question whether the increasing Australian penchant for locking up more and more prisoners in often appalling conditions, for protracted periods of time without meaningful employment, does anything to reduce the crime rate.

It seems to me that these conditions breed vicious and intractable criminals. While there are some adult and youthful offenders who require substantial periods of imprisonment – the seriously violent offenders, for example – most do not fit this profile and could easily be dealt with by non-custodial punishments.

Though all Australian jurisdictions have a great number of alternatives to prison – community service orders, probation, attendance centres, home detention and so on – our rate of imprisonment has skyrocketed in recent years. Yet we have systematically disbanded educational and work programs within prisons that might equip people to reintegrate into society. Instead, we usually send prisoners back into the world with little money and no chance of obtaining a viable job.

Much is made of a few demonstration 'community conference programs' that are operating across the country, particularly with juveniles and Aboriginal people. Here, a meeting is held between an offender and the victim of his or her offence. The purpose of the meeting is to discuss the offence and negotiate an agreement satisfactory to both parties. Evaluations of these programs have been very positive.

So has the experience of some European countries with innovations like trade unions for prisoners, weekend live-in visits by wives and girlfriends, and work release during the day. Crime rates have not increased and neither has the fear of crime.

As long as our politicians, with the active support of sections of the media, persist in calling for harsher and harsher penalties and more and more imprisonment, community conferencing and other non-custodial alternatives will fail to make more than a small dent on the rate of imprisonment.

Cuts to the threshold test for legal assistance and an increased fear of crime and terrorism will ensure that imprisonment remains the dominant approach to crime and punishment in this country. But we will never obtain more than temporary safety if we rely solely on incarceration and, in the process, ignore social justice and equity.

FIONA WRIGHT

Fiona Wright is a restaurateur, entrepeneur and mother to two beautiful daughters, Jessica and Georgina. She lived variously in Sydney, the snowfields of Thredbo and at boarding school in Canberra as a girl, and all these places continue to play important roles in her life. Fiona returns regularly to Sydney, drawn by the beauty of its harbour where she once sailed with her father, skis every winter at Thredbo, and lives in Canberra, where she owns a restaurant by the lake, and several cafes. She is married to Tony, a journalist and author.

DAD

It hadn't been a good week. It hadn't been a good year for that matter. My family had moved house from Thredbo to Canberra and I had become a day girl after several years boarding at an all-girls' school.

No more skiing every day in winter, no more riding my horse and camping out in summer. No more village boys to flirt with at Friday Flat, our swimming hole during those hot mountain summers. Everything had changed.

The new house was in the sticks, a new suburb of cheap housing for young families. Not close to the city like the other girls in my class. A brand new suburban primary school, full of the local kids, and the high school only had Form 1 and 2. It was growing with the rest of the community.

The bus rides to town and school were mostly hot and endless through that first summer. Not a cool look. I cried all the time. My eyes were always swollen, my nose ruby red. I longed for my old life.

Just last summer, Mum and Dad had packed me and my five brothers and sisters into the Valiant, hitched up the biggest caravan you have ever seen and headed north to Queensland. Mum was pregnant with yet another baby, due in a few months.

The family dog and adopted cat with her six kittens came too. Mum could not bear to leave the cat; it wasn't ours, it just moved in and stayed. Dad gave the kittens away at every service station we came to. The mother finally escaped into the cane fields south of Tully during a lunch stop. We smuggled the animals into the caravan parks amidst fits of giggles. With so many kids in the car who would know?

Dad was a yachtsman, and a big business man who was used to doing business in the big end of town in Sydney. He met my Mum and asked her to marry him on the first date.

He drove those endless miles to Queensland so my Mum could visit her father for Christmas. Dad worshipped my Mum and once wanted to buy a house boat and take her around the world on it. I was only seven at the time and it gave me night-mares thinking I would be stuck out in the ocean on a house boat. She loved him and I reckon she would have gone on that house boat

In Cardwell that Christmas of '69 we met with our cousins, six of them from my Mum's only sister. Twelve kids sat down to the Christmas table that year with my Aunt and Uncle, my Mum and Dad and Grampy.

At night we sat around listening to the adults talk, laugh and argue. Mum and her sister were trying to get my Gramps to give up cigars; Narnie, my grand-mother, had just died from lung cancer and Mum and Aunty Valia were hell bent on getting him to look after himself better.

Dad, I think, was mostly bemused, because Aunty Valia smoked like a steam train. But that was then.

School had become difficult those last few months of '69; I was miserable. My eldest sister was always out and she and Mum argued a lot. Simon the baby had been born prematurely and had lots of health prob-lems. He was always in hospital, or so it seemed. Mum had to spend most of her days with him. I wanted her attention but she seemed distant and pre-occupied.

I was thirteen and miserable. School had just finished for the summer break. We were going on another Queensland trip in the Valiant, towing the caravan, but it was not going to be the same.

Three nights before we left my life changed.

I had again cried myself to sleep, listening to the Top Forty on the radio, when I was woken by my Dad sitting beside me on the bed. We talked for hours about how it upset him that I was so sad.

He told me to be strong and help my Mum with the kids. 'She needs you,' he said. He stroked my head and helped me stop crying. He told me he loved me very much and that he would always be there for me.

In the morning when I woke, I was happier than I had been for months. I had seen Dad, who had died three months before. I believe my dad visited me that night. For the rest of my life it has puzzled me, as I do not believe in life after death.